Aṣhtanārī Sandēśaya

Poetical Message through Eight Damsels

අෂ්ටනාරි සන්දේශය

Bandara Bandaranayake, PhD

Aṣhtanārī Sandēśaya

Copyright © 2023 Author Bandara Bandaranayake

First Print, 2023

After making due reference to the name of the author and the title of the book, any part of this book may be quoted or reproduced for academic purposes.

Proposed Reference:

Bandaranayake, Bandara. (2023). Aṣhtanārī Sandēśaya: Poetical Message through Eight Damsels. Melbourne, Australia.

ISBN: 9780645213331

Bandaranayake Consulting Services Pty Ltd

Melbourne, Australia

Dedication

To my beloved sisters:

BM Sumanā Kumārihāmy & BM Karunāwathie

This book has also been published in Sinhala language:

අෂ්ටනාරී සන්දේශය: යුවතියන් අට දෙනකු රැගෙන ගිය කාව්‍ය පණිවිඩය.
මෙල්බර්න්, ඕස්ට්‍රේලියාව. 2023

About this publication

Aṣhtanārī Sandēśaya, "a poetical message through eight damsels", is a book of poetry found written on palm-leaf[1] manuscripts or *puskola poth* in Sri Lanka in Sinhala language.

This work was composed by a poet who lived at Mæṭioḷuva village in Sath Kōrale[2] towards the early period of the Kandyan Kingdom (1469 to 1815 AD). The purpose of this Sandēśaya (message of plea) was to wish Ulagalla Disāwa, a chieftain of Hurulu Palāta in Nuvarakalāviya[3], well, and to urge blessing of holy deities for the release of lands and territories of his ancestral inheritance.

The messengers of eight young women (damsels) travelled nearly 100 Kilometres from Nāthagane village (in Sath Korale), adjoining to the poet's village, to Gaṭulāgan Vihāra (currently known as Thalagulu Vihāraya) in Nuvarakalāviya (Anuradhapura District), which is close to Ulagalla's mansion, to deliver the message of the plea.

I collected palm-leaf manuscripts of this Sandēśaya, compared and analysed them. This effort enabled me to assemble potentially a credible version of the original Sandēśaya . The final outcome is this publication. Now it is presented to local Sri Lankan and international readers for the first time.

A brief literary appreciation of the Sandēśaya revealed that the poet who emerged from a humble village in Sath Kōrale, had the understanding of the subtle nature of this auditory medium (Sandēśa poetry), creativity, poetic insight and language proficiency. I observed

---

[1] Palm-leaf manuscripts are also known as ola-leaf manuscripts.

[2] According to current administrative demarcations this area belongs to Kurunegala District.

[3] According to current administrative demarcations this area belongs to Anuradhapura District.

the poet's capacity to elicit images, feelings and meanings in the listeners' minds by employing effective styles including figures of speech and rhythmic qualities of the Sinhala language.

Curiously, the story behind this Sandēśaya unravels a political struggle faced by chieftains of South Indian descent (Dravidian) in Nuvarakalāviya. Ulagalla Disawa represents an ancestry of South Indian origin who won honorary names and chieftain positions with awards of lands and territories from the king Buvanekabahu of Dambadeni Kingdom (1220 to 1345 AD). A significant portion of South Indian migrant families of the elite, who moved to Sri Lanka during the medieval times, settled in Sath Kōrale and Nuvarakalāviya and eventually absorbed themselves into Sinhala Buddhist society (Bandaranayake, 2021, 2022).

The Sandēśaya starts from the village of Nāthagane, the capital city of the Mundukondapola regional kingdom (which encompassed Sath Kōrale) to which many families of the South Indian (Dravidian) elite flocked seeking chieftain positions and lands for settlements during Kotte and Sithawaka period (Bandaranayake, 2021 and 2022). This Sandēśaya gives an insight into their ongoing struggle to maintain their power and privileges.

By the time this Sandēśaya was written (in early 17th century) the power and privileges of Ulagalla ancestry seemed to have been dislodged and it was felt necessary to seek divine intervention for the restoration. It appeared that many chieftains in Sath Kōrale and Nuvarakalāviya, who particularly had South Indian affiliation, expressed solidarity with the Ulagalla cause. They sponsored the pageant that carried the Sandēśaya along the route to Gaṭulāgan Vihāre.

It is an intriguing factor to note that Aṣhtanārī Sandēśaya is not only a modest piece of poetry but also a story of an illusory ancestry.

Table of Contents

Dedication · iii

About this Publication · v

Table of Contents · vii

Acknowledgments · ix

Chapter 1 · Source of Aṣhtanārī Sandēśaya · 1

Chapter 2 · Introduction to Aṣhtanārī Sandēśaya · 9

Chapter 3 · Classical Sandēśa Kāvya Tradition · 23

Chapter 4 · Sandēśa Kāvya Tradition and Expansion in Sri Lanka · 29

Chapter 5 · Reasons for Selecting Eight Damsels for Aṣhtanārī Sandēśaya · 37

Chapter 6 · Aṣhtanārī Sandēśaya - Travel Route and Parade Design · 49

Chapter 7 · Literary Appreciation of Aṣhtanārī Sandēśaya · 59

Chapter 8 · Concluding Comments · 77

Chapter 9 · Aṣhtanārī Sandēśaya and Comparison with Manuscripts · 83

Appendix 1 - Distribution of Stanzas Among Manuscripts and Overlap · 135

Appendix 2 - System of Transliteration · 143

Appendix 3 - References and Bibliography · 145

Appendix 4 - About the Author · 151

Acknowledgements

I acknowledge many people who supported and encouraged me to complete this publication.

Firstly, I would like to acknowledge two of my friends, Udula Bandāra Oushadhahāmy and RSWM Kumāra Bandāra, for their enormous support. Udula was instrumental in expanding the horizons of my thinking about Aṣhtanārī Sandēśaya and enhancing my imagination of the final outcome of this project, since the very first day of explaining my idea about this project to him. He provided feedback on the structure and contents of the publication. He kindly designed the book cover. Kumāra provided a relentless support, under difficult circumstances, spending many hours reading and discussing the English version of the draft and helping to bring it to the final phase of the publication.

Rangana Kuruwita volunteered to read and fix grammar and usage of Sinhala language in the Sinhala version of the publication. His assistance was instrumental in bringing the Sinhala version of the publication to the final phase. He also supported in making suggestions on comparative analysis of manuscripts.

Rathnasiri Arangala (Sri Jayewardenepura University) encouraged me to complete this publication providing useful references and guidance to conduct comparative analysis of palm-leaf manuscripts. He also read the Sinhala version and made valuable comments to improve its flow and clarity.

EM Sunil Bandāra, Shakila Rājakaruna, Kapila Bandāra Wammbatuwewa, Hasitha Chāmikara Gunasinghe (Kelaniya University), YM Dharmasena Bandāra, AM Herath Bandā

(Pohoravatta) helped me to collect historical ola-leaf manuscripts. Jinadasa Dannansuriya (Kelaniya University), Sāgarika Herath (Provincial Council, North-Western Province), Ukkubandā Karunānanda (Kelaniya University), and Chirān Windsor supplied valuable references.

The people who helped me to explore the current remnants of the historical layer of Ashtanārī Sandēshaya were Māminiyāwe Ilangasinghe (APB Ilangasinghe), Venerable Valpola Vijitha (Sri Vāpikārāmaya Vihāre, Palugolla), Venerable Mahanelubæve Rathanasāra (Thalagulu Rajamahā Vihāre or Gatulāgan Vihāre, Galkulama), Venerable Udabōvala Ariyadamma (Sri Sucharithwardhanārāmaya Vihāre, Mædagamuva), Venerable Polgahavela Vijitagnāna (Sri Sudharmārāmaya Vihāre, Diddeniya), UB Disānāyake, Dilrukshi Priyadarshani (Ugā Ulagalla Resort), Sāvithri Pānabokke, Udeni Bandāra Ilangasinghe, WM Piyathilaka and Githāni Samarawikrama.

I would like to thank Chandra, my wife, for her patience with the decades of my journey to pursue academic interests.

Finally, I extend my respect and gratitude to the poet of the original Aṣhtanārī Sandēśaya from Mætioḷuva and other poets who followed his footsteps. I acknowledge the Silpādhipathi clan and the residents of the village of Mætioḷuva (present Mædagamuva) for unknowingly represent such a grand heritage.

I regret if I have failed to mention the others who helped me in numerous ways. Without all your support this publication would not have been a reality.

The final decisions on the content of this publication are my own and any shortcomings do not reflect on those who helped me.

Bandara Bandaranayake
Melbourne, Australia. 2023

Chapter 1:

Source of Aṣhtanārī Sandēśaya and Comparative Methodology

This chapter introduces the source of Aṣhtanārī Sandēśaya manuscripts written in Sinhala language and outlines the manner in which manuscripts were compared and finally stanzas were presented. A comprehensive introduction to Aṣhtanārī Sandēśaya and this publication is presented in the next chapter.

Manuscripts collection

I obtained three digital images of original ola-leaf manuscripts of the Sandēśaya - one manuscript kept at the British Library (Number OR 1166 (114)) and two other manuscripts kept at the Sri Lanka Museum (catalogue numbers 2175 and 2176). A handwritten copy of an ola-leaf manuscript was also obtained from the village of Pohoravatta in Kurunegala District. All the four manuscripts describe the messengers who journeyed from Nāthagane in Kurunegala District to Gaṭulāgan Vihāre in Anuradhapura District to deliver the Sandēśaya.

I also came across a 1909 publication which presents another version of Aṣhtanārī Sandēśaya. The carriers of this Sandēśaya journeyed from Nāthagane to Diddeniya Devala (shrine of gods) in Kurunegala District, a different destination, for a different purpose.

The following section describes the details of each manuscript including its exterior appearance, content, and format.

1. **Aṣhtanārī Sandēśaya, an ola-leaf manuscript held at the British Library (abbreviated as BL in this publication). The British Library record is OR 1166 (114).**

This manuscript was obtained from the Hugh Nevill Collection at the British Library. It has two sided 14 leaves (pathra - පත්‍ර) with 27 pages of text. Diameter of each of the leaves is 4.2 cm x 44.4 cm. Each side contains four quatrains totalling 108 (27x4) verses.

The numbering of leaves is shown in numerical order (1 to 14) and Sinhala alphabetical order form "ka" ක to "kau" කෞ The first text page of the leaf has been referred to as 1a and the back page of the same leaf as 1b. I have used this sequence in this publication to maintain the consistency of reference.

The origin of this manuscript is unknown. There is no reference to the person who has copied it into ola-leaves or where it was collected in Sri Lanka by Hugh Nevill.

In this manuscript, the Sandēśaya starts from Nāthagane in Kurunegala District and ends at Gaṭulāgan Vihāre (temple) in Anuradhapura District.

2. **Aṣhtanārī Sandēśaya, the ola-leaf manuscript held at Sri Lanka Museum (abbreviated as M1 in this publication, Sri Lanka Museum record 2175).**

This manuscript contains 20 ola-leaves (pathra - පත්‍ර), including the front and back pages. The front page shows the title while the back page provides the details of the person in whose possession the original copy was, who copied it, and when it was copied to ola-leaves. The dimension of each page is 30.48 cm (12 inches) by 6.35 cm (2 and half inches). Each ola-leaf page contains 6 verses which add up to 108 (18 x 6) verses.

According to the back page, the original manuscript was held by Mātobuwā Kōrāla of Hurulu Palāta. It had been copied into ola-leaves by a person named Kīrthirathna[4] on 12 August 1898.

There is no numbering on pages of the original manuscript. Therefore, I used 1.1 to refer to the first verse on the first page and 1.6 to refer to the last verse on the first page in this publication and six verses will be sighted here.

In this manuscript, the Sandēśaya starts from the village of Nāthagane in Kurunegala District and ends at Gaṭulāgan Vihāre in Anuradhapura District.

3. **Aṣhtanārī Sandēśaya, another ola-leaf manuscript kept at Sri Lanka Museum (abbreviated as M2 in this publication, Sri Lanka Museum record 2176).**

This manuscript is similar to M1 but it is a different manuscript. It also contains 20 ola-leaves including the front and back pages. The front page shows the title while the back page provides the details of the person in whose possession was the original copy, who copied it, and when it was copied to ola-leaves. Dimension of each page is 30.48 cm (12 inches) by 6.35 cm (2 and half inches). Each ola-leaf page contains 6 verses totalling 108 (18 x 6) verses.

This manuscript was held by Mātobuwā Kōrāla of Hurulu Palāta. The person who copied is not stated but it had been copied on 21 February 1897.

There is no numbering on pages of the original manuscript. Therefore, I used 1.1 to refer to the first verse on the first page and 1.6

---

[4]   U W M Kirtiratne was a clerk for H C P Bell, Archaeological Commissioner. He copied many palm leaf manuscripts from original collections (Silva, WA, 1938).

to refer to the last verse on the first page in this publication and six verses are given here.

In this manuscript, the Sandēsaya starts from Nāthagane and ends at Gaṭulāgan Vihāre.

4. Aṣhtanārī Sandēsaya manuscript found at the village of Pohoravatta (abbreviated as PV in this publication). This handwritten manuscript had been copied from an ola-leaf manuscript.

This manuscript was in the possession of AM Herath Banda at the village of Pohoravatta, in Polpithigama Divisional Secretariat, Kurunegala District. According to him, the condition of the original manuscript was deteriorating, and his father had copied only 83 legible verses around in 1940's. These verses (83) had been collected from Herath Banda and published by YM Dharmasena Bandara in his book "Nikawagampaha Kōrale Athithayen Bindak" in 2011.

This manuscript is an incomplete Sandēsaya as some of the initial verses and final verses are absent from it. Moreover, there are five new verses describing new landmarks on the route. These five verses do not appear in BL, M1 and M2.

The verses have been numbered in this publication as PV 1 to PV 83.

5. Aṣhtanārī Sandēsaya, 1909 publication, by M D Dāmpi Appuhāmy (abbreviated as A1 in this publication).

This version of Aṣhtanārī Sandēsaya was obtained from ola-leaf manuscripts and published by MD Dāmpi Appuhamy in 1909. It was reprinted in "Sankha" magazine published by the Department of Cultural Affairs, Sri Lanka, in 2004 (volume January - June 2004). The text of this Sandēsaya for the publication in Sankha magazine was prepared by KB Herath.

This 2004 publication erroneously introduces that it starts from Nāthagane and ends at the Kataragama Devala dedicated to Sanda

Kumaru at Handapāngama near Uyanwaththa in Kurunegala District. But the content of the poems reveal that it starts from Nāthagane, but it ends at Diddeniya Devala in Ihala ōthota Kōrale in the same District. The aim of this Sandēśaya was to seek blessing for the eight young women who carried the message.

This Sandēśaya has 76 stanzas out of which 40 stanzas look similar to Aṣhtanārī Sandēśaya that leads to Gaṭulāgan Vihāre. Eighteen (18) additional stanzas describe the landmarks (up to Handapāngama) including one stanza describing a new village. Those 58 stanzas have been incorporated in this publication[5].

The stanzas are listed in this publication as A1.1 and A1.2 etc.

6. Aṣhtanārī Sandēśaya. From Nāthagane to Kataragama Devala (gods shrine dedicated to Sanda Kumaru) at Handapāngama near Uyanwaththa. (Abbreviated as A2 in this publication).

Sannasgala (1964, p585) refers to an Aṣhtanārī Sandēśaya that travels from Nāthagane to the Kataragama Devala at Handapāngama near Uyanwaththa in Kurunegala District. I was unable to find this manuscript for my review. The place from where Sannasgala discovered this copy is not clearly stated.

Similar other Nari Sandēśayas

7. Nārisath Sandēśaya, 1909 publication, by HB Andirishāmi, Kandy (abbreviated as N1 in this publication).

This Sandēśaya was written by a poet called Silpādhipathi in 1833. It is carried by seven damsels from Nāthagane to Dambulla Vihāre. I had

---

[5]   The 18 stanzas that were excluded from this publication include the five stanzas at the beginning, four stanzas describing the Diddeniya Devala and nine stanzas at the end explaining the purpose. The 58 selected stanzas were considered as common to, or new, or copies or reflections of Aṣhtanārī Sandēśaya that leads to Gatulāgan Vihāre.

access to a printed version of this Sandēśaya by HB Andirishāmi of Kandy in 1909. According to the introduction, several ola-leaf manuscripts were collected, compared and edited for the publication of Andirishāmi. I was unable to find the original ola-leaf manuscript. This published version has 152 stanzas.

8. Nari Sandēśaya (abbreviated as N2 in this publication).

The Sri Lanka Museum catalogue refers to a "Nari Sandēśaya " (catalogue number 2247) in its collection. This catalogue entry (2247) states that was a poem composed as a message sent through a woman to a deity at Dambulla Viharaya. I was unable to find this manuscript at the Museum due to a potential misplacement. It can be a completely different Sandēśaya or a different version of the Nārisath Sandēśaya.

Comparison of manuscripts and presentation

The total number of stanzas relevant to Aṣhtanārī Sandēśaya is 131. Chapter nine presents the collection of these stanzas.

The identification of stanzas was based on manuscripts of BL, M1 and M2. They each contained 108 stanzas. I believe these three manuscripts are based on the original poem. Later, five new stanzas from PV and 18 new stanzas from A1 have been added. The poets who added new stanzas might have believed that they were enhancing the value of Sandēśaya. Any other particular reasons to add new verses to the original poem of Aṣhtanārī Sandēśaya are discussed in chapter 2 as applicable.

The manner in which all these five manuscripts overlapped and interconnected are provided in appendix 1.

Column 1 in Chapter nine provides the serial number of each stanza (1 to 131) while the column 2 presents all the stanzas of Aṣhtanārī Sandēśaya collected for this publication in original Sinhala language followed by its English version in the system of transliteration. The list of transliteration is given in appendix 2.

Language and style differences

The British Library manuscript (BL) appears to be neat, and it uses a more scholarly Sinhala language. The M1 and M2 are similar in content but have some minor differences in wording and spelling. As the PV had been repeatedly copied, slight changes have occurred in the original verses. Consequently, some words and stanzas appear different and imply different meanings. A1 has emerged as a new version of Aṣhtanārī Sandēśaya. Since A1 has been printed and published, some changes could have happened as a result of editing and therefore, the occurrence of some new refined words and lines are unavoidable.

The language differences (stanzas, lines, words, or spelling) in each manuscript are presented in footnotes. These footnotes explain the differences found in each manuscript.

No attempt was made to correct the accuracy of words and spellings. I find that Aṣhtanārī Sandēśaya has many words and usage whose meaning is beyond comprehension of reader, because the diction seems to represent a bygone era. The poem had been composed within a non-sophisticated social environment and the mastery of language of the poet represents the particular era.

The stanzas are presented in this publication in the exact way they appear in the manuscripts to aid the readers to understand the historical nature of its language and style.

Headings and sub-headings are used for the benefit of the readers. The headings introduce each section while sub-headings describe landmarks on the route of the Sandēśaya.

Chapter 2:

Introduction to Aṣhtanārī Sandēśaya

Purpose of this publication

The purpose of this publication is to present Aṣhtanārī Sandēśaya, a less known Sri Lankan historical Sandēśa Kāvya (message poem) to an international readership. This publication will help to introduce and preserve Aṣhtanārī Sandēśaya for future generations.

I acknowledge that I have a personal relationship to the cherished memory of this Sandēśaya. I grew up listening to random verses of this Sandēśa Kāvya as they long survived in my local folklore in Nikawāgampaha Kōrale in Kurunegala District. That was because the travel path of the Sandēśaya ran through the locality of my native village. Some landmarks in my home area such as "Galgiriya Kanda", "Galgiriya Vǣva" "Boravǣva", "Dembatōgama" and "Rambewa" have been praised highly in the Sandēśaya. Since these stanzas eulogizes local identities the Sandēśaya has been committed to memory of the local residents. Therefore, they survived in the local memory.

Pohoravatta is a village in my home area where a manuscript (PV) was preserved.

Having heard random verses of this Sandēśaya, I had developed an interest since my late adolescence to conduct research to find out its original ola-leaf manuscripts, various versions, its place in the Sri Lankan poetry, its historical and sociological value, and its literary value. I was determined to revive it and share it with a wider readership. So, this is the final outcome of my interest and determination.

What is the content of Aṣhtanārī Sandēśaya?

Aṣhtanārī Sandēśaya tells a message carried by eight damsels from the village of Nāthagane in Kurunegala District to Gaṭulāgan Vihāraya in Anurādhapura District, seeking blessing and divine protection for Ulagalla Disāwa (a Chieftain who ruled from Ulagalla division of Hurulu Palāta) in Anurādhapura District, and also seeking blessing to regain his lost land and inheritance.

The time frame in which this Aṣhtanārī Sandēśaya was written is not yet agreed upon, but it could fall into the period just after the Sithawaka/Kotte kingdom (1412 to 1597 AD) or the early period of the Kandyan Kingdom (1469 to 1815 AD). I would like to provide my assumptions for this time frame in the latter part of this chapter.

Nāthagane is situated in current Bamunākotuva Divisional Secretariat in Kurunegala District (in the North-Western Province) while Gaṭulāgan Vihāra (currently known as Thalaguru Vihāre[6]) is situated in Thirappane Divisional Secretariat of Anuradhapura District (in the North Central Province). The journey of the message takes approximately 100 Kilometres celebrating over 85 locations that have

---

[6] There is no vihara with the name of Gatulāgan Vihara. In "Ceylon in 1893" by John Ferguson in 1893 lists Gatalagama Mountain situated 10 miles south-east of Anuradhapura. Talaguru Viharaya is situated close to Gatalagama mountain.

been acknowledged along the way. Each place has been praised by beautiful verses.

Godakumbura (1953, page x) states that Aṣhtanārī Sandēśaya starts from Nāthagane and ends at Kataragama shrine in Diddeniya village of Ihala Mōthota Kōrale of Hiriyala Hathpattuwa in the same district of Kurunegala. However, Sannasgala (1964, p585) states that the version he saw describes a journey of eight women from Nāthagane to Handapāngama Devala of Uyanwaththa in the same district of Kurunegala.

Hugh Nevill (1955, p245) states that Aṣhtanārī Sandēśaya starts from Nāthagane and ends at Gaṭulāgan Vihāra in Anuradhapura (SVP3 p245). He collected this ola-leaf manuscript from Sri Lanka and added to his grand collection of ola-leaf manuscripts that was kept at the British Library[7].

Aṣhtanārī Sandēśaya follows the tradition of message poems popularised by the epic Meghadūta composed by Kālidāsa (4 to 5 century AD). However, by the time Aṣhtanārī Sandēśaya was written, Sandēśa Kāvya had evolved into different forms and purposes. A brief introduction to the tradition of Sandēśa Kāvya, its history and how this literary branch evolved in Sri Lanka is provided in the next two chapters.

The author of the Sandēśaya and where he lived

The verse No 3 (Chapter 9) hints that the author is a renowned poet from the village of Mæṭioḷuva in Pihiti Rata. There is no clue about his name. However, he has seen the great King Edirisingha.

'පින්පෙත් යුත් ඉදිරිසිංහ රජවර බැළ   ව

මණ්මත් මෙත් සිරි නිසර බඳ සිරි සිළ   ව

පැන්පත් වරණ විතරණ යන එළ නෙළ   ව

නන්ලත් ගොත් පිහිටි සිටි රට මැටිඹළ   ව

---

[7]   For this publication, a digital copy of this manuscript was obtained from the British Library.

> pinpet yut idirisinha rajavara bæḷuva
>
> manmat met siri nisara baṅda sirisiḷuva
>
> pænpat varaṇa vitaraṇa yana eḷu neḷuva
>
> nanlat got pihiṭi siṭi raṭa mæṭioḷuva'

The village Mæṭioḷuva borders the village of Nāthagane in the current Bamunākotuva Divisional Secretariat of Kurunegala District, from where the eight damsels started off on their journey carrying the message. The king Edirisingha is believed to be the king Edirimannasuriya who succeeded his brother, the King Irugal Bandara. Both of them were the rulers of Mundukondapola Regional Kingdom of Sath Kōrale (Kurunegala District) under Sithawaka/Kotte kingdoms during the 16th century. Their royal palace is believed to be situated at Nāthagane (Bandaranayake, 2021, page 56-57).

The poet known as Silpādhipathi who wrote another Sandēśaya called Nārisath (seven damsels) Sandēśaya is believed to hail also from this Mæṭioḷuva village. It suggests that Aṣhtanārī Sandēśaya is also one of his creations (Godakumbura, 1953, P x). The poet was an astrologer and a Ganithāchārya (mathematician) who had the expertise in drumbeating and conducting traditional Hindu religious ceremonies and rituals. Godakumbura (1953, p ix) states that this author or another contemporary author has written Aṣhtanārī Sandēśaya, due to the similarities in both creations. It is not clear whether the Nārisath Sandēśaya or Aṣhtanārī Sandēśaya was first to be created.

The traditional occupants of Mæṭioḷuva village represent the Nakathi/Berawā caste which excels in performing drums, dancing and rituals at religious ceremonies. Ancestorial surname of Mæṭioḷuva residents' is Silpādhipathi. However, the residents of Ethalapitiya and Kandegāra, the two neighbouring villages of Mæṭioḷuva, also currently use the surname of Silpādhipathi. In any case, this surname seems to be commonly used among the Nakathi professional caste. This means, apparently, the author had belonged to this particular professional community group.

Because of the nature of the services rendered by the Nakathi professionals, they had the opportunity to familiarise themselves with or excel in the knowledge and skills of astrology, literary languages like Pali and Sanskrit, Hindu culture, rituals related to Yāga and Hōma, and slokas and mantras. This professional background and its influence could have naturally inspired creative individuals in this clan to be poets and artists (e.g. Bharana Ganithaya who wrote Nilakobō Sandēśaya in the middle of the 18th century, was from this caste group).

However, it appeared that the endurance of this professional group was curtailed by the aspirations of the modern world which undervalued the traditional caste-based professional identity. It has been construed that this profession as socially lowly in the modern society. The name Mæṭioḷuva used to remind its inhabitants of their caste being regarded as lowly. Therefore, the residents opted out to change their traditional surnames. Moreover, they changed the village name to Mædagamuva around 2010.

This transformation has signified a shift of a value system. The village and its traditional inhabitants moved into a new phase which made the professional inheritance of the village disappear gradually. I find that none of the current inhabitants knows about this glorious and distinguished poet Silpādhipathi who was one of their celebrated ancestors.

Who was Ulagalla Disawa?

As stated elsewhere, the aim of the Sandēśaya was to seek blessing for Ulagalla Disāwa of Hurulu Palāta[8], in Nuvarakalāviya[9] (of

---

8   Ulagalla is a well-known historical village that has been well preserved to date in Anuradhapura District.

9   It has been recognised as this area is the coverage of Nuwara Wewa, Kala Wewa and Padaviya Veva. But Maminiyave Ilangasinghe (interview evidence)

Anuradhapura District). The Sandēśaya reveals that Ulagalla was a descendent of the ancestry of Ilangasinghe Kalu Kumāra. There is a high praise about this chieftain including his illustrious ancestral possessions which include his ancestral Manson (vimana), wealth, power and privileges in the verses from 118 to 122 (refers to Chapter nine).

Historical ola-leaf manuscripts stand as a useful source of information to identify the chieftains who lived in Ulagalla location in the past. For example, Vanni Upatha manuscript (Obeyesekere, 2005, page 23-26), identifies seven princes who migrated to Sri Lanka during the Dambadeni Period (1220 -1345 AD). The King Buvanekabahu 1 (1271–1283 AD) of this kingdom settled them in various parts of the country. Two princes who originated from Madurai (Madurapura) royal family were settled in Ulagalla area in Anuradhapura. One of them known by the name of Kalu Kumara Bandara was awarded with twelve villages including Kaluwila. He was honoured as "Kalu Kumara Vanniyā". The other prince, Ilangasinghe Bandara was given nine villages including Kattaman Kulama, and he was honoured as "Ilangasinghe Vanniyā." Kaluwila is situated 3km towards north-west of current Ulagalla village, and Kattaman Kulama is situated 3km south-east of present day Ulagalla. The Ilangasinghe Kalu Kumaru mentioned in Aṣhtanārī Sandēśaya can be either of these two or a descendent of them.

Another piece of historical information about the local chieftains in Ulagalla area is contained in Mukkara Hatana ola-leaf manuscript (Bandaranayake, 2022, page. 182-186). When South Indian Mukkarus invaded Sri Lanka during the Kotte Kingdom, the King Parakramabahu the VI (1412-1467 AD) brought in Karaiyars soldiers from South India (Bandaranayake, 2022, page. 182-186) to fight the invaders. After Mukkara invaders were defeated by the Karaiyars

---

thinks this Nuwarakalawiya is larger than even the current Anuradhapura District.

soldiers, they were allowed to settle in Sri Lanka. They were also employed to train the local royal army. Vanni Upatha manuscript (Obeyesekere, 2005, page 23) provides a list of local army leaders who were trained by them. Among them were Halkande Vædirāla, Morakæve Gamarāla, Maminiyāve Vædi Gamarāla, and Ulagalla Vædirāla. When the Portuguese started a power base in Trincomalee, Ulagalla Vædirāla organised Vædi fighters from his locality to fight the Portuguese. Therefore, as Vanni Upatha states he was awarded a number of villages and conferred a Vanniyā (Vanniyar) post by the King of Kotte in recognition of his services. A copper plate (Tamba Sannasa) was inscribed with the details about the award.

This information suggests that Ulagalla Disāwa can be a descendant of either Kalu Kumāra Bandāra or Ilangasinghe Bandāra or Ulagalla Vanniyar; all of whom were related.

Why Ulagalla needed blessings?

Verses 130 and 131 reveal the intention of the Sandēśaya was to win back the land and the division (rata) which had been graciously given to Ulagalla ancestors by the King Buvanekabahu of Dambadeni Kingdom. There could have been an ancestral land dispute and this Sandēśaya was one solution to the dispute. The Sandēśaya also pleads with deities of Gaṭulāgan Vihāre to bring freedom, peace and happiness to Ulagalla Disawa (chieftain).

මවා නික සිතින් එළ පද පතල ක   ර

පෑවා සේක බුවනෙක අදහසින් ක   ර

පාවා දීපු රට තොට පට පහස් ක   ර

බෝවා ආසිරින් මා නිදහසක් ක   ර

mavā nika sitin eḷu pada patala kara

pǣvā sēka buvaṇeka adahasin kara

pāvā dīpu raṭa toṭa paṭa pahas kara

bōvā āsirin mā nidahasak kara

'නරනිඳු බුවනේක යන නම නිරිඳු වෙ   ත

පුර ඉඳු සඳ සිසිර ගොත් කැළුමෙන් දිමු   ත

සුරණිඳු කරුණු කුළනින් රට දෙවු වෙ   ත

පරසිදු උලගල්ලේ මැතිඳුට වේය සෙ   ත

naranidu buvaṇēka yana nama niriṅdu veta

pura iṅdu saṅda sisira got kæḷumen dimuta

suraṇiṅdu karuṇu kuḷunin raṭa devu veta

parasidu ulagalle metuduṭa vēya seta

The information suggests that Ulagalla was a Disawa or an area chieftain who wielded power and leadership, but his authority had been somehow disputed.

What were the reasons for the dispute? I present the following analysis for the potential reasons for the dispute and the loss of privileges of Ulagalla Disawa in early Kandyan period (early 17th century).

The verses from 118 to 122 recite about Ulagalla water reservoir (*Væva*), Ulagalla village and the Ilangasinghe Kalu Kumara's mansion, his inherited wealth, privileges and heritage. Then goes on to bless Ulagalla Chieftain without clearly identifying any relationship to Ilangasinghe Kalu Kumara lineage and heritage. It is reasonable to assume that Ulagalla was none other than one of Ilangasinghe Kalu Kumara by descent. He had been identified as the Disawa (royal administrator) who ruled from the Ulagalla locality by the time of the Sandēśaya .

As referred elsewhere, there had been historical land grants and award of authoritative positions to a number of migrants in the Nuvarakalāviya province from the time of Dambadeniya era (1271–1283 AD).

During the Kotte Kingdom (1412-1467 AD) one Malala prince had been given the Anuradhapura region and named Nuwarawawe Suriya Vanni Kumārasinghe Bandara (Bandaranayake, 2021, p124). It appears that this Kumārasinghe Bandara was more powerful as he had the privilege of being the custodian of Atamasthāna at Anuradhapura holy city[10]. In addition, he was in charge of Kaluwila region which had previously been given to Kalu Kumara Bandara during the Dambadeniya period. He also held the "Mahā Vanniyā" position to whom many Vanniars and other local chieftains reported to.

Vanni Vitthiya (Bandaranayake, 2021, page 99) manuscript suggests that during the Kotte period potentially the power and authority of the descendants of Kalu Kumara Bandara and Ilangasinghe Bandara had been disturbed or dislodged. However, from time to time the descendants of Kalu Kumāra Bandāra obtained vanniyār positions, but had to report to Kumārasinghe Bandara Maha Vanniyā chieftains. This new authoritative position, administrative structure and land awards resulted in a drawback to Kalu Kumara clan.

What was the setback to Ulagalla clan?

According to Davy (1821) and D'Oyly (1912), the area between Jaffna kingdom and Kotte kingdom was named Vanniya and it was divided into eighteen pattu (sub-districts). Nuvarakalāviya was under a Disāwanni (a division of Maha Disawa)[11] during the Kandyan kingdom but this chieftain was regarded as a junior Disawa (Sulu Disawa)[12] compared to the other Disavannies of Kandyan Kingdom (e.g. Sath Kōrale and Sathara Kōrale).

The person who ruled Nuvarakalāviya under a Maha Disawa was called "Mahā Vanniyā." He held the custodianship of eight sacred places of Buddhists (Atamasthāna). Eighteen Vannivaru reported to

---

[10] According to Karunananda, 2005, pg. 11, the history of Nuvara væva family commences from the legendary Prince Bōdhiguptha who brought sacred Sri Maha Bodhi (Bo tree sampling) to Sri Lanka during King Devanampiyathissa (247 BC to 207 BC).

[11] For example, in 1815, this Disāvanni was under the control of Galagoda Disawa, who was the Maha Disawa.

[12] Karunananda, 2005, Nuwarakalawiya, pg. 11.

this Mahā Vanniyā. Karunananda (2005) says that the Mahā Vanniyā posts were always filled by the Nuvara Væva family of Anuradhapura. There is no doubt that Nuvara Væva clan was superior to the chieftains in Ulagalla area whose land inheritance goes back to Dambadeni era.

The royal status of Nuvara Væva family was further strengthened during the Kandyan kingdom. "Madurapuren ā Vittiya" manuscript (Bandaranayake, 2022, p146-147) refers to a fascinating story about a group of princes and princesses from the Madurai royal family who came to Sri Lanka during the Kandyan kingdom and stayed at Nuvara Væva valawuva on their way to Kandy. One princess called Suparna became pregnant due to a secret affair with Tikiri Banda, a son of Nuvara Væva valawuva family, during their short stay. Therefore, she married Tikiri Bandā and her brothers went to Kandy and obtained royal positions at the Kandyan royal palace. As a result of this new connection the Nuvara Væva family became more powerful and influential.

The award of the Kaluvila rata (during the Kotte Kingdom) to the Malala prince Kumārasinghe Bandara of Nuvara Væva which was previously held by Kalu kumara Bandara or Ilangasinghe Bandara (from Dambadeniya period) hints about the dislodge of traditional land ownership and privileges of Kalu Kumara clan. The transfer of the same land areas or ratas to new chieftains, redrawing of boundaries together with the appointment of new chieftain positions by the king were common in medieval times. On some occasions local chieftains appealed to the king not to reallocate their ancestral lands and countries (rata) to new chieftains (Bandaranayake, 2021, p126) as they wanted to retain their ancestral land and their inheritance.

Aṣhtanārī Sandēśaya can be a humble and subtle way of pleading with the god to aid to remedy the injustice that had transpired to Ulagalla ancestry. The poet of Aṣhtanārī Sandēśaya made a supplication to deities at Gaṭulāgan Vihāre to bless Ulagalla matindu to regain the lands given to his ancestors during the reign of King Buvanekabahu of Dambadeniya.

When was Aṣhtanārī Sandēśaya written?

There is no agreement on the time in which Aṣhtanārī Sandēśaya was written. Godakumbura is of the opinion that this poet had lived circa AD 1883 and Aṣhtanārī Sandēśaya belongs to 19th century. Sannasgala (1964, page 585) also thinks that it belongs to the Kandyan era. However, Hugh Nevill believes that Aṣhtanārī Sandēśaya was composed between 1540-1560 because the poet had seen King Edirisingha (Edirimannasuriya) of Mundukondapola regional Kingdom.

There is no reference to the Mundukondapola regional kingdom in the Sandēśaya even though it starts from Nāthagane where the royal palace was located. I believe that the original Aṣhtanārī Sandēśaya was written early in the Kandyan Kingdom after the collapse of the Mundukondapola regional Kingdom in 1597 (Bandaranayake, 2021, p63-64). It is possible that the poet had seen King Edirimannasuriya (who ruled from 1540 to 1560) and lived even after the collapse of the kingdom.

Kaluwila region was given to the Malala prince, Kumārasinghe Bandara of Nuvara Væva during the Kotte Kingdom which collapsed in 1597 and this land dispute of Ulagalla clan be obvious in the early Kandyan period to seek assistance.

I believe that the Sandēśaya had a number of versions with updates starting from the early 17th century to the late Kandyan era. PV and A1 can be such versions. PV includes five stanzas that describe new villages - Kiralā Gedara (verse 67), Palugassæva (verse 68), Karambē Pidivilla (verse 72), Boravæva (verse 88) and Kandulugamuva (verse 92) - in the travel path of Aṣhtanārī Sandēśaya towards the north of Sath Kōrale. It suggests that the author of this version was from the north of Sath Korale where Pohoravatta is situated. The poet of A1 has added 18 new stanzas[13] to add value to the 11 villages[14] that have already been described in original Aṣhtanārī Sandēśaya. The poet of A1 could possibly belong to the Mætioḷuva generation.

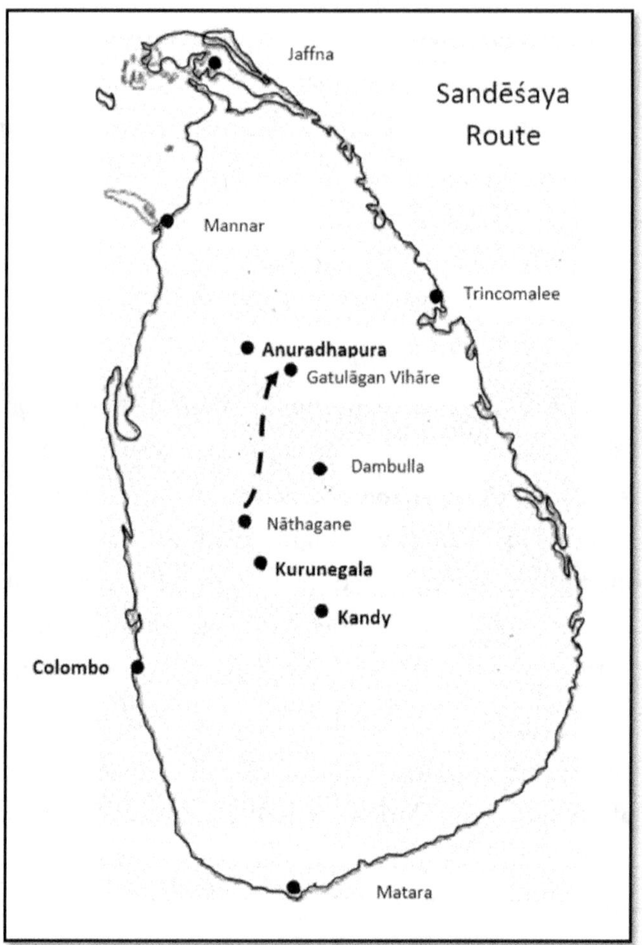

Map 1: Sandēśaya Route

---

[13] The serial numbers relevant to these new stanzas in this publication are: 24, 25, 30, 32, 36, 37, 45, 46, 47, 51, 53, 55, 57, 58, 60, 62, 63, and 64.

[14] The villages that had already mentioned in BL, M1 and M2 but added additional poems in A1 were Kollægala, Yaddessākanda, Dolu Kanda, Vællāgala, Alupothaganvela, Tissovela, Sērugolla, Nuwara Kanda, Māguruoya, Nindagama and Diwulvæva.

What is the current status of Ulagalla clan and Ulagalla Mansion?

Ulagalla family belongs to a historical lineage, as stated elsewhere, they originated from a few noble families who migrated from South India during the Dambadeni period. These South Indian migrants were assimilated into Sinhala Buddhist community and spared into other parts of the country (Bandaranayake, 2021). This clan's power base was shifted from time to time. Some descendants still live in the locality including the villages like Ulagalla and Maminiyāwa[15].

As stated elsewhere, Nuvarakalāviya was under a Mahā Vanniyā mainly represented by the Nuvara Væva family. Karunananda (2005 p160-163), provides a list of chieftains who reigned Nuvarakalāviya during the British rule from 1815.

Accordingly, the "Mahā Vanniyā" (chieftain) of Nuvarakalāviya from 1815 to 1833 was Nuwarawawe Suriya Kumara Mudiyanse. In 1833, Nuvarakalāviya was divided into two divisions, namely Eastern Division (Hurulu Palāta) and Western Division (Nuwaragam Palāta), each in charge of a Mahā Vanniyā. Ilangasinghe Kalukumāra Thamaravæva Banda Mudiyanse (related to Ulagalla clan) was in charge of the Eastern Division from 1833 to 1839. Nuwarawawe Suriya Kumārasinghe (related to Nuwara Væva family) was in charge of Western Division from 1833 to 1836.

In 1839, Nuvarakalāviya was divided into three divisions (Hurulu Palāta, Nuvaragam Palāta and Kalāgam Palāta) and each division was in charge of a Raṭe Mahathtayā (a chieftain position).

---

[15] I would like to acknowledge that I captured only notable chieftains in the area in this publication as relevant to its subject matter. However, their descendants either still live in this area or expanded to other parts of the country. Further, their surnames were changed when they had only daughters who took their husbands surnames.

From 1839 to 1878, there were three Raṭe Mahathtayās for Hurulu Palāta to which the Ulagalla area belonged. Two consecutive Raṭe Mahathtayās were represented by Ulagalla clan – namely Ilangasinghe Kalu kumara Thamaravæva Banda Mudiyanse from 1839 to 1848 and Ilangasinghe Kalukumāra Rajakaruna Nikavæva Mudiyanse from 1849 to 1877. In 1878, Nikavæva Loku Bandā was appointed to the Raṭe Mahathtayā position of Hurulu Palāta (Karunananda, 2005 p160-163). Nikavæva elite family was linked to Ulagalla clan by marriage in late 1800's.

One descendent of Ulagalla family was Anula Kumarihamy who was the only daughter of a (Ulagalla) Raṭe Mahathtayā. She became the owner of the Ulagalla mansion. She married Kiribandā Pānabokkē who was from Kandy. Kiribandā renovated the Manson in 1915 and after that it was known as Pānabokkē Valavuva. During the civil war in 1980's Anuradhapura became a military town and the valavuva was taken over by the army as their headquarters.

Pānabokkē family sold the Ulagalla Valavuva to Ugā Escapes Management (Pvt) Ltd of Sri Lanka in 2007 to transform it into a tourist hotel. Now the valavuva is a luxury hotel and known as Ugā Ulagalla Resort.

This hotel nestles in a sprawling 58-acre lush green garden of ancestral Ulagalla land with over 200 year-old mansion in its centre. The old section of the valawuva has an impressive façade, large masonry columns at ground level supporting a balcony with slender timber columns at the upper level creating a fascinating composition.

The hotel preserves its rich traditional architecture, cultural heritage and historical significance.

The next chapter presents an introduction to the classical Sandēśa Kāvya tradition.

Chapter 3:

Classical Sandēśa Kāvya Tradition

This chapter presents a brief introduction to Sandēśa Kāvya literary tradition[16] in order to help the readers to understand the position Aṣhtanārī Sandēśa holds in the broader scope of the Sinhala Kāvya (poetry) literary tradition. It will also help to understand if the Aṣhtanārī Sandēśa has deviated or distanced itself from the classical tradition.

What is a Kāvya? This auditory literary medium, which includes both poetry and prose, is characterised by rhythm and abundant usage of figures of speech such as metaphors, similes, personification, hyperbolic expressions (amplifications) to create its distinctive emotional effects[17]. The result is a short lyrical work, court epic,

---

[16] Kāvya refers to the Sanskrit literary style used by Indian court poets flourishing between c.200 BCE and 1200 CE (Macdonell, Arthur Anthony (1900), "Kāvya or court epic", A History of Sanskrit Literature, New York: D. Appleton and company)

[17] A highly artificial Sanskrit literary style according to the Encyclopedia Britannica,

narrative or dramatic work. Aśvaghōṣa (c. 80–150 AD), a philosopher and poet considered to be the father of Sanskrit drama, is attributed for coining the term (Macdonell, 1900, p 335, Gonda, 1984, p6-8).

The format of Sandēśa Kāvyas consists of a message, a messenger (or bearer or a dūta) who carries the message, and a recipient or a place where the message is delivered to. All Sandēśa Kāvya have a similar format apart from the diversity of the carriers. It is recognised that the carrier should belong to a high caste or be a superior being (Thilakasiri, 2013, p15). The title of the Sandēśaya usually derives from the name of the bearer of the message.

All Sandēśa Kāvya share common set of characteristics which include:

- giving a warm welcome to the messenger
- praise of the messenger
- mention of the recipient of the message
- praise of the city of departure and the lord
- instructions on start of the journey
- explanation of the itinerary
- description of the recipient and the residence
- direction to convey the message with the blessing on the messenger (Thilakasiri, 2013, P14-15).

There are instances where the poet is likely to deviate slightly from the traditional format depending on the purpose and the subject matter.

Kālidāsa's Meghadūta was the defining moment of the popularity of this literary tradition. It is regarded that Meghadūta was written in the 5th century AD. Subsequently many poets, who were inspired by the work of Kālidāsa, had written Sandēśa Kāvyas imitating Kālidāsa in his content, style and metre (beats).

Meghadūta belongs to the category of classical poetry as it essentially exhibited both high degree of quality and the ability to staying in power (stay in memory of the reader). Poems included in the list of classic poetry have both of these characteristics (McKinsey, 2023).

Meghadūta's emotional subject matter, the poetically elevated standards and the depth of the poetic style made Meghadūta more enticing. Meghadūta illustrates the sorrowful life of a Yaksha, a servant of Kubera, the king of Alakapura who is considered to be the god of wealth. Yaksha was separated from his wife, he was alone on the mountains of Chhota Nagpur. "Emaciated and melancholy, he sees, at the approach of the rainy season, a dark rainy clouds moving northwards. The sight fills his heart with yearning, and impels him to address to the cloud a request to convey a message of hope to his wife in the remote Himalaya" (Macdonell, 1900, page 335). This work became an ideal, stimulating and passionate literary model for the other poets.

The aspect of love described in a messenger poem is not "love in union" (sambhogasrrigara) but "love in separation" (virāha) which is more passionately appealing.

We must assume that the messenger poem is a well-established category of Kāvya even before Kālidāsa's time. Kālidāsa might have taken some inspiration for his poems from a part of Valmiki's Ramayana and other classical poem with a different structure. Therefore, we can surmise that he had previously been familiar with dūta Kāvya before he composed Meghadūta. In Rāmayana, Rama sends his faithful Hanumanth as a messenger to his abducted wife Sita in distant Sri Lanka (Gonda, 1984 page 114). Eventually Rāvana was defeated by Rama in a battle. Love triumphs after persistence, dedication and goodness after intense separation.

Gonda (1984 page 113) suggests Sandēśa Kāvya began in the category of Khand Kāvya (small poem). This classical form shows the following elements: the poem opens with two young people of opposite sex, very much in love, who, due to some misfortune (curse as in Meghadūta) get separated. One of the two is abducted, the other partner undergoes painful separation, in order to ease the pain of separation the lover sends the beloved (or vice versa) a long message, the contents of which are generally given in the poem. As Gonda explains, this separation can be interpreted either as erotic nature or the remoteness of man from god, the desire of the lonely woman for reunion with her lover (Gonda, 1984 page 113).

It was the usual practice in early poetry to choose a monsoon cloud as a messenger since the rainy season provides the most productive background from the artistic point of view. This background was very suitable for invoking an atmosphere of unhappy love and separation if the lover failed to return. It would therefore seem quite natural for poets to choose a monsoon cloud as the most fitting messenger. We may surmise that this was the favourite dūta figure in early messenger poetry and in this respect Kālidāsa and others were merely following their predecessors (Gonda, page 125)

It can be said that a wide variety of animals, natural phenomena, etc. appear as messengers both in worldly and religious and (or) moralistic Dūta Kāvya. Sandēśa poets selected messengers like objects (e.g. pavana – wind; megha - cloud), or internal entities and qualities like mind and characteristics, or birds with noble qualities and of noble rank. However, the critics say that it is fruitless and not justifiable to use objects and birds as dūta as they cannot talk or explain messages (Thilakasiri, 2013). However, whether the bearer is living or nonliving or superior intelligent being is immaterial as long as figures of speech are effectively employed to enrich the meaning and bring out sensual emotions in the work of poetry.

Versions of Meghadūta

The total number of stanzas in Meghadūta varies between 110 and 130. According to Macdonell it has 115 stanzas (1900, P 335). It seems probable that the great popularity of the work led to a number of versions. This is indicated partly by the fact that there is a Tibetan translation of 117 stanzas, a Sinhalese version with 118 stanzas and a work by Jinasena with 120 stanzas (Gonda, 1984, page 116). It is important to highlight that there was some influence to create different versions of Aṣhtanārī Sandēśaya by other poets.

Spread of the Sandēśaya tradition

The messenger poem tradition later evolved with two names to refer to them. While North Indian poets predominantly used the name of Dūta, the name Sandēśaya became popular among the South Indian poets. It is curious to observe that many poets had used the same dūta for different purposes of Sandēśa. For example, in Indian literature, there are two Pavana dūta, three Hansa dūta, three Chandra dūta, five Magha dūta, six Mano dūta, three Kokila Sandēśa , three Shuka Sandēśa , and three Hansa Sandēśa (Thilakasiri, 2013). However, their time periods are not clearly stated. After Meghadūta (cloud), the oldest Sanskrit dūta to be employed, was Pavana dūta (wind).

There are a number of Sandēśa Kāvya written in Kerala and Tamil Nādu of South India. The oldest Sandēśa Kāvya in South India was written in Sanskrit by Laksmidāsha in Kerala (1100 AD). That is Shuka or Girā Sandēśaya. Hansa was written by Vedanta Dæsika in 1268 (in Kerala) following the Meghadūta model. Kokila written in the 15th century by Uddanda is about a message from a young man to a maiden. In addition, Mayura Sandēśaya and Brunga Sandēśaya were written respectively by Udaya and Vasudeva in the 16th century (Thilakasiri, 2013).

There were Sandēśaya s composed in Dravida, Kannada and Malayalam languages during the 17th and 18th centuries. Their main objective was to display religious devotion or bhakti. The oldest and the most creative Sandēśaya in Malayali was Unnunila Sandesham. This followed the Kālidāsa model as the message was sent by a young man from Trivandrum to his lover in Kodungaluraya. The messenger was a prince named Adithyawarma (Thilakasiri, 2013).

The popularity of Sandēśaya is evident in North India and South India following Kālidāsa's masterpiece. The next chapter provides a brief account of its spread in Sri Lanka.

Chapter 4:

Sandēśa Kāvya Tradition and Expansion in Sri Lanka

Political agendas for Sandēśa Kāvya in Sri Lanka

Sandēśa Kāvya seemed to have evolved in a different path in Sri Lanka. The "love in separation" that elicit erotic sentiment was not the focus in Sinhala Sandēśa Kāvya. The focus had been shifted to promote and celebrate favourite rulers and to serve the self-interests of poets. Sandēśa Kāvya in Sri Lanka has fertilised with political motives from the beginning.

The oldest Sandēśa Kāvya found in Sri Lanka was Mahānāgakula or Mānavulu Sandēsaya written in Pali during Polonnaruwa era (1153-1186). This was sent to Sangharakkitha, a chief monk of Arimaddanapura in Burma. The dūta was a person named Gnāna and the purpose of the Sandēsaya was to inform the chief monk to encourage King Siridamma in Burma to do religious changes similar to those done by King Maha Parakramabahu in Sri Lanka. Mānavulu Sandēsaya was a reply to an ashna that was brought by Gnāna to

Nāgasena chief monk at Mahānagakula Ramba vihara (Thilakasiri, 2013, p25).

Mayura Sandēśaya is considered to be the first classical Sri Lankan Sandēśaya written around 1370 AD. It intends to invoke blessing from God Vishnu on King Buvanekabahu V. The blessing is extended to the king's wife named Jayasiri, Alagakkonara the second-in-command, and Alagakkonara's brother Dewasvami. The aim of the poet was to highlight the greatness and heroism of Alagakkonara than the King Buvanekabahu V (Thilakasiri, 2005 p 22).

Thisara Sandēśaya was written around 1407 AD by the chief incumbent of Devundara vihara. Its purpose was to seek blessing of God Vishnu to bring peace and happiness to King Parakramabahu of Dætigampura.

Paravi Sandēśaya (1430-1445) and Salalihini Sandēśaya (1450 AD) seem to have a hidden agenda to stop Prince Sapumal, adopted son of Parakramabahu VI, becoming the successor. Paravi Sandēśaya was written to seek a suitable husband for Princess Chandrawathie, the elder daughter of the King Parakramabahu VI. This Sandēśaya was also aimed at seeking divine intervention to bless this couple with a son who could succeed the King. It appears that the King, the Palace and the Kings counsellors were not in favour of Prince Sapumal becoming the king (Thilakasiri, 2005, p38). However, the Princess Chadrawathie died unexpectedly. Salalihini Sandēśaya was written (1450 AD) to plead with God Vibhishana for a son for Princess Ulakudaya, another daughter of King Parakramabahu VI.

Girā Sandēśaya (1415 AD) and Hansa (1415 AD) were written to wish great King Parakramabahu VI well. Kokila (1460-1467 AD) was written to seek protection for Prince Sapumal during his invasion of Jaffna regional kingdom (Thilakasiri, 2005; 2008). All these Sandēśaya have political purposes.

Evolution of Sandēśa Kāvyas during and after Kandyan Era

A number of Sandēśayas were written during the Kandyan period. Among them were Kahakurulu, Katakirili, and Nīlakobo (Danansuriya, 2008). The Nīlakobo was written by Barana Ganitha Guru. He lived during reigns of Kirthi Sri Rajasinghe (1747-1780) and Rājadhirājasinghe (1780-1798). The purpose was to seek blessing of Kandakumaru to cure the author's illness. Another minor Sandēśa was Diyasævul written by Ven Thalarambe Dhammarakkitha, seeking of blessing from god Kataragama to heal an illness in his foot. It appears that the purposes of Sandēśaya have been changed from concerns for others benefit to self-benefit.

Kirala Sandēśaya was written by a monk named Ven Dēvamiththa at Malwaththa Vihara. The purpose was to seek blessing for Ehelepola from the god Sanda Kumaru at Ambekke Devala. Ven Dēvamiththa seemed to have had hostile attitude towards the foreign king Sri Wikrama Rajasinghe who ruled from Kandy at the time.

There are nearly 100 Sandēśa Kāvyas have been written since the 19th century. Their themes vary from encouragement of pilgrimage and condemnation of corruption and violence to expression of fun and sarcasm. Danansuriya (2008) identifies that ordinary people became poets during and after Kandyan Era. There were ordinary monks, naides, ganithachāryas, āchari bavalath among the authors and the poets.

Aṣhtanārī Sandēśaya was written in Sath Kōrale of the North-Western Province. Scholars like Ven Demammada Sumanajothi, PB Sannasgala and Godakumbura and Hēvāvasam have paid attention to literary work produced particularly in the North-Western Province (Danansuriya, 2008, p 1211). The literary work proliferated in Sath Korale during the Kandyan period as these areas were not affected by the European influence. It is reasonable to say that the common theme of this style of poetry was to promote Buddhist religious awakening.

All these literary products have been simple, honest, and their subject matter covered a broader area (Danansuriya, 2008, p 1211).

Categorisation of Sandēśa Kāvya in Sri Lanka

Popular Sandēśa Kāvyas in Sri Lankan have been divided into two categories on the basis of their literary quality, namely major Sandēśa Kāvya and minor Sandēśa Kāvya. 'Mayura', 'Thisara', 'Parevi', 'Kokila', 'Salalihini', 'Girā', 'Hansa' and 'Saul' fall into the category of major Sandēśaya Kāvyas. Other Sandēśayas like 'Kaputu', 'Nīlakobo', 'Kahakurulu' etc. which were written later regarded as minor Sandēśaya Kāvyas. Aṣhtanārī Sandēśaya is categorised as a minor Sandēśaya Kāvya.

Pilgrimage poems

Some Sandēśa Kāvyas that were written during the Kandyan era have been named as pilgrimage poems (vandanā kāvya).

After Kīrtisri Rajasinghe started reconstructing viharas and dagabas, there was a dawn for pilgrimages to historical religious places. Pilgrimage books were written and Kāvyas were composed following the visits to these newly constructed, renovated or ancient places of worship. Pilgrimage is a trip, often a long one, made to a holy place for religious reasons. Such places were considered special, where people would go to show their respect.

According to Sannasgala (1964, p584-586), examples of such pilgrimage Kāvyas were Samanala Hæli, Bōmada Alankāraya, Jayamahābōdhi Wandanāwa, Samanala Wistharaya, Sripādavandanā Gamana etc. Sannasgala (1964. Pages 584 to 586) suggests that both Nārisath and Aṣhtanārī Sandēśayas belong to the category of pilgrimage poems. Venerable Horana Vajirajnana (1992, page 308 to 310) also agrees with this idea. Sannasgala believes that Silpādhipathi poet of Mæṭioḷuva wrote Nārisath Sandēśaya and a few other pilgrimage poems.

Nārisath Sandēśaya

I would like to give a brief account of Nārisath Sandēśaya in this context. It is similar to Aṣhtanārī Sandēśaya as the bearers of the message are young women. There are other similarities as well. Both Aṣhtanārī Sandēśaya and Nārisath Sandēśaya may have a interrelation since both originate from Nāthagane. At least some versions of both Sandēśayas can be the works of the same poet or descendants of Silpādhipathi generation at Mæṭioḷuva.

A number of scholars comment on Nārisath Sandēśaya. All of them of the opinion that the Sandēśaya starts from Nāthagane in Sath Kōrale and goes to Dambulla Viharaya in Sathara Kōrale (Sannasgala's 1964, p585; Godakumbura,1990 p 229, and 1953, Page x; Vajiragnana, 1992. page 310; and Sumanajothi,1966, page 28). They do not provide comments on different versions of Nārisath Sandēśaya except from the disagreement on the number of stanzas of this poetry.

I have observed the copy of Nārisath Sandēśaya published by HB Andirishami in 1909. The Sandēśaya clearly states that it was composed by a poet named Silpādhipathi from Mæṭioḷuva. Therefore, the authorship of this manuscript is unarguable.

The structure and the presentation of this Sandēśaya is different from that of the classical Sandēśa tradition. It starts with a "Mārga Ashna" section which is a poetical textual style known as Vurtaganda sāiliya (Vajirajnana, 1992, p210). Andirishami (1909, p 5) recognises this part as the "surname" of the Sandēśaya which was followed by the poems version of the Sandēśaya. Both text and poems versions were destined to Dambulla vihara. It is not clear whether they (text and poem versions) were two different works written at different times put together later and given the same title.

I observed that both versions (text parts and poems part) have highlighted different locations on the way to Dambulla via northern part of Sath Kōrale. For example, the locations stated in the text part is largely different from the poems part. The poem part has more locations listed. The shortest possible way that leads to Dambulla should be via Ibbagamuwa, Mælsiripura finally entering Sathara Kōrale (in the Central Province) where Dambulla is situated.

The poet prefers a slightly longer route covering a large part of northern Sath Kōrale via Bamunākotuva, Vāriyapola, Nelliya, Daladāgama (Maho), Uduveriya, Randenigama, Dematagolla, Nettipolagoma, Galgiriyāwa, Madagalla, Dambe, and Kahalla to reach Dambulla finally. The route of the messengers that enters Nuvarakalāviya and leads to Sathara Kōrale where Dambulla is situated is not clear. Whether the messengers had entered Nuvarakalāviya via Siyambalangamuwa or via Dambe and Herathgama crossing the Pallekæle Wildlife Sanctuary to reach Kahalla is not clear. The only clear reference made to the entry of Nuvarakalāviya is the mention of Kahalla and the place from where the messengers saw Ritigala mountain in the distance.

No landmarks close to Dambulla are mentioned. This is probably because of the poet's lack of knowledge about the topography of the last leg of the journey. However, many verses have been allocated to praise the elegance and holiness of Dambulla vihara (Rathnagiridamba Parvataya) and its sacred shrines of gods (devala).

It appears that the poet intended to elevate prime locations of Sath Kōrale in his poems to express his allegiance to the Sath Kōrale where he celebrated his life.

The Sandēśaya starts venerating triple gem, a ritual different from other Sandēśayas. Next, the manner in which the seven women prepared for the journey is presented in elegant stanzas (from 2 to 36). The seven damsels start the journey after begging protection from Goddess Paththini (stanza 37). Stanzas 38 to 105 describe the locations on the way to Dambulla Rock temple. The format and the rhyme scheme have been formed in such a way to rhyme with the names of the villages along the route.

All the temples on the way to Dambulla have been venerated with offerings of sacred gifts (puja). Stanzas 106 to 135 are allocated to describe the grace of Dambulla and its surrounding with the request to damsels to worship with utmost respect and devotion.

It is hardly surprising that Dambulla cave monastery was selected as a destination of a Sandēśaya. Dambulla cave monastery remains as the best-preserved ancient edifice that has never have been abandoned in the history of Sri Lanka. King Valagambā of Anuradhapura ((103, 89–77 BC) is thought to have converted the caves into a vihara.

Stanzas from 146 to 148 describe the reflections of the damsels about the pilgrimage and the request made to the poet (stanza 144) to compose the poetry.

The pilgrimage took seven days during the month of Vesak (May) (stanza 9) and the poem was composed after two months in the month of Esala (July) (stanza 151). Stanza 150 states that the poem was composed by Silpādhipathi Ganithāchārya of Mætioḷuva and the stanza 151 states that it has 152 verses.

The last four stanzas reveal the poet's reflections on his task and the merits he expected from the completion. In stanzas from 145 to 148, the poet boasts that he is a celebrated poet and a Ganithāchārya from Mætioḷuva and he desires best wishes and the protection from the divine gods. Ultimately, with the stanza 152, he wishes that he will attain Buddhahood with the merits that he accumulates from this divine creation.

As already identified, Andirishami (1909) publication of this Sandēśaya has 152 stanzas. Godakumbura (1953) agrees with Andirishami about that number. Sannasgala (1964) attests the Nārisath Sandēśaya has 150 stanzas while Vajiragnana (1992) accepts it has over

150 stanzas. All these accounts confirm that the poetry has been updated by other poets or at least it has more than one version.

Vajiragnana (1992, p 208-210) thinks the Mārga Ashna section shows the competence and the creativity of the poet. The style of the writing has certain pattern to make it audio friendly. Vajiragnana thinks this section presents the ability and the depth of the Sinhala language to employ text poetically.

Vajiragnana thinks that the quality of the poem is with a limited literary appeal. So, this Sandēśaya lacks Kāvya taste and can be regarded as a new Sandēśaya tradition that shaped a new face of padya creation (Vajiragnana 1992, 308 to 310).

The next chapter presents an analysis of the reasons to select young women as messengers and eight of them.

Chapter 5:

Reasons for the Selection of Eight Damsels for Aṣhtanārī Sandēśaya

Use of humans and in particular female messengers are uncommon in the Sandēśa Kāvya tradition that was elevated by Kālidhāsa. It appears that Nārisath and Aṣhtanārī Sandēśaya are the only Sandēśayas[18] in Sri Lanka that used female messengers. Was it really unplanned and accidental or intentional? The aim of this chapter is to investigate the potential reasons leading to select young women; particularly eight of them.

Erotic sentiment

It is to be emphasised that in single-stanza love poetry in classical Indian literature, female (dūti) played an important part (Gonda, 1984, p114) eliciting erotic sentiment or *sringāra rasa*. Sringāra is the first of

---

18   Sri Lanka Museum also has another Sandēśaya called "Nari Sandēśaya" Catalogue Number 2247 which was not available for review.

the nine rasas[19], usually translated as erotic love, romantic love, or attraction or beauty (Manamohan, 2002; Pollock, 2016; Wikipedia). Rasa means "flavour", and the theory of rasa is the primary concept as well as the driving element behind the classical Indian arts including theatre, music, dance, poetry, and sculpture.

The rasa concept without any doubt has a universal humanistic appeal. However, there is criticism that the Indian literary appreciation has given the highest place to Rasa rather than other poetic elements like Alaṅkāra (figures of speech), Guṇa[20], Rīti[21], Vṛtti[22] and Pravṛtti (local usages) etc. The relevance of all these elements has been examined with reference to their usefulness to the Rasa. It is believed that the poets who attained perfection in depicting Rasa have been considered to be of high calibre in Indian literature (Chaturvedi,1996, Ray 2022); for example, Vālmiki and Kālidāsa who had attained the mastery of eliciting rasa.

---

[19] Bharata Muni articulated eight Rasas in the Nātyasāstra, an ancient Sanskrit text of dramatic theory and other performance arts, written between 200 BC and 200 AD. They include 1. Śṛṅgāraḥ (romance, love, attractiveness),2. Hāsyam (laughter, comedy), 3. Raudram (fury), 4. Kāruṇyam (compassion, mercy), 5. Bībhatsam (disgust, aversion), 6. Bhayānakam (horror, terror), 7. Veeram (heroism), 8. Adbhutam (wonder, amazement) (Manamohan, 2002). A ninth rasa - Śāntam rasa (peace or tranquillity) was added by later authors (Pollock, 2016).

[20] Ten guna in Kāvya 1. (ojas) strength, 2. (prasāda) clarity, 3. (śleṣa) firm structure, 4. (samatā) sameness of evenness of sound, 5. (samādhi) metaphorical expression, 6. (mādhurya) sweetness, 7. (saukumārya) gentleness, 8. (udāratā) elavatian, 9. (arthavyakti) perspeouity, and 10. (kānti) beauty. (Source: www.wisdomlib.org/definition).

[21] Rīti – is an indispensable characteristic feature of a poem, for an arrangement of words or syllables, which render help in heightening the excellence of rasa. It consists in the special arrangement in combination of words and the speciality lies in the possession of Guṇas (source: www.wisdomlib.org/definition).

[22] Vrttis or modes of expression, divided into three classes based on the 'aural-effects': primary alliterations classed as elegant (upa-nagarika); ordinary (gramya), and harsh (parashu). (source: www.sreenivasaraos.com/tag/Kāvya-alamkara-sutra-vritti)

Sringāra rasa is found in abundance in the single stanza poetry. The main parts in single stanza poetry are played by the beloved (nayika - female), the lover (nayaka - male), the female messenger (dūti) and the beloved's girlfriend (sakhi) (Gonda, 1994 p65). The most important of these is, however, the nayika, who can appear in any of several female roles. She can be a wife of another man (parakiya[23]), a visitor to the lover (abhisarika[24]), a hetaera or a courtesan (ganikā), a newly-married woman (navodha), a sulky or disdainful woman (manini[25]), and someone who had previously experienced to be in love (praudha), etc. But she may also appear as the lover's own wife (svakiya). Erotic sentiment was an essence of this poetry. The poems collected in the Sattasai (an ancient collection of Indian poems in Mahārashtri Prakrit language) describes two forms of love: Sambhoga[26] and Vipralambha[27], or happy and unhappy love respectively (Gonda, 1984, p65). Therefore, erotic sentiment extended to eliciting emotional feelings of both happy and miserable love.

Sringāra rasa is discouraged in Buddhism. Buddhist teachings suggest that sensual pleasures in general, and sexual pleasure in particular, are a hindrance to the practice of jhāna (wisdom) and to reach liberation or enlightenment. The Buddhist ideal of love is manifested as loving kindness (mettā) towards all beings.

Nārilathā concept

The Buddhist mythology relates a story about a mythical climber (climbing plant) called "Nārilathā" in Himalayās that blossoms a flower that resembles a woman of exquisite beauty and grace. The flower is said to have the power to distract even ascetics in meditation. This

---

[23] Parakiya means love not by marriage life, by friendship or a mistress or wife of another.

[24] Means one who is engaged in love.

[25] A lady who is strong and powerful in her deeds, strong minded.

[26] Means carnal enjoyment, sexual union, copulation.

[27] The sense of unrequited longing that is an exquisite pain.

mythical flower in Thailand, is called "Nāreepol" and in Sri Lanka, it is called "Liyathambarā" (Wikipedia).

One Buddhist story narrates that an ascetic who had been meditating deep in the jungle for many years, on having seen one of these flowers renounced his spiritual achievements in favour of a worldly life. Ananda Coomaraswamy has reproduced this story in his Mediaeval Sinhalese Art (page 91) as found in Kathāvastu Prakarana to illustrate the exquisite beauty of the mythical Nārilatā flower. According to the story, a Brahman in Kāsirata lost his dhāyana (concentration power) on seeing Nārilathā flower in spite of the austerities he followed in order to attain the concentration (Dhyana power)[28].

An intricate pattern of vine called "Nārilatā" is depicted in classical paintings and decorations in the Buddhist temples of Kandyan era in Sri Lanka. Nārilathā pattern was a favourite motif (Kumāraswāmy, 1979). One of the most captivating representations is the one found at the Ridi Vihara which is reproduced in Mediaeval Sinhalese Art[29].

Nārilathā is a concept that creates erotic sentiments (or *sringāra rasa*) and artistic creations.

Damsels in Nāthagane

Why were young damsels selected particularly from Nāthagane? Traditional Vitti Poth (ola-leaf manuscripts on historical events) suggest that Nāthagane was an exciting and sophisticated city that enjoyed worldly pleasure at the time or just before the present Sandēśaya was written. The manuscripts provide hints about the worldly and sensual pleasures that the Nāthagane men and women enjoyed (Obeyesekere, 2005, p69; Bandaranayake, 2021, p53-63). Nāthagane was the principal city where the palace of Mundukondapola

---

[28] https://asiseeit2000.wordpress.com/2012/01/29/narilatha-the-flowers-in-sri-lankas-mythology/

[29] Ibid

regional kingdom was located during Sithawaka and Kotte periods (Bandaranayake 2021, p53 to 63). Andirishami (1909, p5) recognises the proud history of Nāthagane saying that it was full of celebrated elites and mudalies (chieftain position holders) who held traditional chieftain positions. Srilak Kada Ayuru manuscript (Obeyesekere, 2005, page 68) states that the people who lived in the city were "Mahā Māni" i.e., they were fanatically proud and arrogant of themselves.

Regarding women this Srilak Kada Ayuru manuscript states that the women who were born there were bursting with "raga", i.e. lived emersed in sensual pleasures. This description suggests that the city was lively and exciting, but its character was unconventional.

This is a capital city to which many South Indian migrants (particularly men) looking for a new way of life were attracted. Among them were many mercenaries. This was a time that many wars broke out and many local men lost their lives in wars. It is possible that many young local women looking for foreign and sophisticated partners were attracted to this city. This breed of women could have been unconventional.

The poet of Aṣhtanārī Sandēśaya must have been familiar with and admiring the life of the women in this locality. Therefore, perhaps it is not coincidental that Nāthagane women were selected as bearers of more than one Sandēśaya that were to dispatch to different locations from this place.

Also, it is unlikely that young damsels were selected mainly for eliciting erotic emotions (sringāra rasa) in poetry. The subject matter of Aṣhtanārī Sandēśaya does not strictly permit it. There are many possibilities. However, eight young women were selected as the bearers of Sandēśaya representing charming groups of family from Nāthagane. This selection had been more appealing not only to exhibit their splendour in procession, but it also helped the poet to praise the sparkling quality, graciousness and natural beauty in poems.

Hindu religious beliefs

Sandēśa Kāvyas often have associations with gods and goddesses whose help or blessings are often prayed for. I would like to disclose at least two South Indian goddesses, Paththini and Lakṣhmi, who became popular because of their benevolence during the Kotte Kingdom and thereafter.

The goddess of Pattini is a guardian deity who protects people from diseases and calamities, and interacts favourably with nature, bringing rains and promoting fertility and the growth of vegetation. Essentially, Pattini represents maternity, purity, healing, and piety embodied in femininity, yet in a divine form. This goddess is the glorified form of the woman Kannaki who lived in India; she was renowned for her chastity (Obesekere, 1984; Embuldeniya, 2018). Pattini is considered a guardian deity of Sri Lanka as recognised in Sri Lankan Buddhism and Sinhalese folklore (Encyclopedia.com, Obeyesekere.1984, Embuldeniya.p, 2018).

There are two theories about the arrival of Pattini in Sri Lanka. One theory is that she arrived in Sri Lanka during the rein of King Gajabāhu 1 during the Anuradhapura Kingdom (Obeyesekere, 1984). According to the other theory, she arrived during the Kotte Kingdom. Furthermore, King Mayadunne, King Sithawaka Rajasinghe, and King Wimaladharmasuriya 1 gave the royal patronage to the cult of goddess Pattini who gets established in Sri Lanka (Embuldeniya.p, 2018). Obeyesekere (1984) states that Pattini had been the most popular deity among the Buddhists of Sri Lanka and the Hindus of the East Coast since the medieval times.

It is to be noted that Hindu beliefs were reawakened among the Sinhalese Buddhists since the medieval periods due to an influx of migrants from South India, particularly from Kerala (Malala Desha) and Madurapura in Tamil Nādu to the territories of the North-western province (Bandaranayake, 2021). Nāthagane, where the palace of the

Mundukondapola kingdom was located, was a centre of attraction to south Indian migrants during the Sithawaka period. During this time both Hindus and Buddhists assimilated the worship and the cult of goddess Pattini. The author of this Sandēśaya and his clan could have been connected to a South Indian migrant group who specialised in Hindu religious rituals and drum beating and the author was respectful of the goddess Pattini.

The Sinhala Buddhist community generally worship Hindu gods and goddesses. One version of Aṣhtanārī Sandēśaya reaches God Kataragama shrine (devāla) at Diddeniya (Sinhala Wishvakoshaya, page 294). The God Kataragama or Kanda Kumaru is a popular god in Sri Lanka. This version of the Sandēśaya seeks blessing for the author. I gather that most of the traditional settlers at Diddeniya were Tamil Hindus who were later assimilated into Sinhala Buddhist community[30].

The version of Aṣhtanārī Sandēśaya, the focus of this publication, reaches a Buddhist temple, Gaṭulāgan Vihāre, seeking blessings. The history of Gatulāgan Vihāre (Thalaguru Rajamahā Vihāraya) goes back to the 2nd century BC. It is said to have been built in the time of king Saddhāthissa (137-119 B.C.) converting the natural caves into a Buddhist monastery. The poet could have selected this vihāre as it was the significant religious centre close to Ulagalla mansion.

It is unlikely that a Buddhist shrine in principle can provide such worldly blessings. I explore that there are two god's shrines in Nāthagane and Gaṭulāgan Vihāre. I gather the Pattini Shrine in Nāthagane is more popular than the Vishnu shrine in the same area. Damsels of Nārisat Sandēśaya starts the journey after worshiping the

---

30   According to interview data collected from the incumbent at Diddeniya Vihāre, many settlers of Diddeniya originally were Tamil Hindus who worshiped God Shiva at this shrine. Followingly the guardianship was transferred to God Kataragama. The Tamil Hindus in Diddeniya later assimilated into Sinhala and became Sinhala Buddhists. Among their current surnames include Kumarasnghe Mudiyanse and Kurukulasuriya Mudiyanse.

goddess Pattini at Nāthagane. Gaṭulāgan Vihāra premises has two shrines. One is devoted to Vishnu. A stature of Vishnu is placed and worshiped at the vihāra chamber. The other is very famous for multiple gods including Bahirava is called Rāmaya. Rāmaya is currently more popular among villagers. That could have been devoted to Pattini at one stage. In any case the Sandēśaya could have been delivered to any of the shrines.

Aṣhtanārī Sandēśaya gives the impression that the damsels started the journey from the Paththini shrine at Nāthagane and ended at another God's shrine at Gaṭulāgan Buddhist vihara following the purpose and the tradition of Sandēśaya poetry.

The Theory of Goddess Lakṣhmi (Ashta Lakṣhmi)

The Goddess Lakṣhmi is another Hindu goddess worshiped in Sri Lanka. This goddess grants both worldly prosperity and liberation from the cycle of life and death.

The Goddess Lakṣhmi fittingly has eight forms, hence the name Ashta Lakṣhmi. Is the concept of Ashta Lakṣhmi subliminally represented in this Aṣhtanārī Sandēśaya? It will be worthy to investigate.

The following are the Ashta Lakṣhmi forms[31].

- *Aadi Lakṣhmi*: Adi Lakṣhmi is Maha Lakṣhmi's first manifestation and stands for welfare and euphoria.
- *Santhana Lakṣhmi*: is the bestower of offspring.
- *Gaja Lakṣhmi*: mythology tells us that Gaja Lakṣhmi brings back the wealth lost by Indra from the ocean. It implies that worship of Gaja Lakṣhmi brings back lost prosperity and wealth.

---

[31]

https://web.archive.org/web/20070212060836/http://www.parashakthitempl e.org/pages/ashta_lakshmi.aspx

- ***Dhana Lakṣhmī*:** she provides abundant wealth.
- ***Dhānya Lakṣhmī*:** while Adi Lakṣhmi is regarded as the incarnation of life, Dhānya Lakṣhmi is worshipped because she represents food that sustains life.
- ***Vijaya Lakṣhmī*:** She is the goddess of victory not only in battle but also in ensuring victory over all hurdles.
- ***Dhairya Lakṣhmī*** (or Veera Lakṣhmi): She bestows courage and strength on those who worship her so that they may overcome all difficulties and stresses in life.
- ***Aishwarya Lakṣhmī*:** she broadly denotes wealth but it also means wealth of good health, knowledge, learning, strength. She generates power or the eight facets of Aishwarya through the Ashta Lakṣhmi.

Among the purposes of Aṣhtanārī Sandēśaya were to seek help to regain lost land and bring good wishes to Ulagalla Disawa. Coinciding with this purpose, Lakṣhmi goddess has eight forms and holds the power to bring back lost wealth. The eight manifestations of Ashta Lakṣhmi possibly fits with the purpose of this Sandēśaya . It is possible that the cultural background and the influence that the poet was exposed to could have compelled him to select eight damsels.

Other reasons

The fact that the traditional Sri Lankan culture recognises the graceful and respectful place the women have in the society goes long way back into the history. This is not from the sensual point of view.

This cultural perception goes back to the period of Kuveni the wife of the Prince Vijaya who migrated at the dawn of Sri Lankan history. Following her death Sri Lankans started a cult of worshiping her as a deity. There are other goddesses and women deities like Pattini and many Biso Bandaras[32]. In the traditional Sri Lankan culture, maidens are recognised as pure and respectable. For example, virgins were given priority at auspicious rituals and practices because of purity reasons.

Buddhism, the religion practiced by majority of Sri Lankans, has stanzas (gāthas) dedicated to respect and worship the mothers (as well as fathers). There are long standing cultural practices like alms giving to mothers (Kiri Amma Dhānaya – alms being given to weaning mothers) as well i.e. mother is considered to be equal to monks.

The folklore narrates that during the reign of King Nissankamalla (Polonnaruwa Kingdom) young women adorned with gold jewellery could walk by herself across the country without being harmed or harassed. This exemplifies that the women were respected, protected and their security was guaranteed in the Sri Lankan traditional culture.

Further, there have been many queens reigning in Sri Lanka throughout the history. This country has also produced the first woman Prime Minister in the world. The respect for women and the recognition of them in high esteem have been a common practice in the history.

Therefore, the selection of young women to carry a precious message in a Sri Lankan Sandēśa Kāvya cannot be denied.

Is there any significance using young women - eight of them?

It is logical at this stage of the publication to explore the reasons as to why "Ashta" or eight damsels were selected and whether there is any customary significance of this number. As explored in the previous section, it is possible that there was an association with Ashta Lakṣhmi

---

[32] The Goddess Tara worshipped as the consort of Avalokitesvara, also known as Biso Bandara, her image, made of stucco, is housed together with the Bodhisattva in a single shrine. The sculptures seem to belong to the Kandyan period - 1529-1815 A.D. Refers to http://www.dlir.org/archive/orc-exhibit/items/show/collection/10/id/12513

that leads to the selection of eight damsels for the purpose of the Sandēśaya, however, none of the theories can be verified.

At this stage, I would like to draw readers' attention to a few artistic forms where "naris" have been represented in paintings and sculpture. These artistic forms range from the group of four to nine. Ananda Kumaraswamy in his work "Madyakālina Sinhala Kala" (Medieval Sinhala Arts, 1979, pages 89 to 92), refers to various nāri related artworks and images found at religious places like Ridi Viharaya (Dodangalanda, Kurunegala). Examples: Chaturnāri Palanquin (a god image house carried by four women), Panchanāri Ghataya (vase or container with five nāri images around it), Shadnāri Thorana (pandol) (the entrance decorated with six women figures to a religious place), Sapthanāri Thurangā (Horse with seven women images), Aṣhtanārī Rathaya[33] (vehicle with eight women images), Aṣhtanārī Ghataya (vessel or vase with eight women images), and Navanāri Kunjaraya (nine entwined maiden figures in the shape of an elephant).

We are unable to clearly establish the reasons for using eight women in this Aṣhtanārī Sandēśaya . The groups of nāris used in art works range between four and nine. Ashta does not seem to have clear connection to the subject matter in hand. It is also possible that the number had no particular cultural appeal.

The next chapter presents an analysis of the route of the Sandēśaya. It expresses particular historical, political and sociological reasons, if there are any to select this route, the shape and the form of the travel composition.

---

[33] Sinhala Vishwakōshaya (second volume, page 294) states that in fact it has only seven images of women. The image in the middle is Kamadeva (Hindu god of love and desire).

Chapter 6:

Aṣhtanārī Sandēśaya - Travel Route and Parade Design

The messengers of Aṣhtanārī Sandēśaya (also of Nārisath Sandēśaya) start from the village of Nāthagane and travel along specific paths selected by the poet. It appears that the paths were not the shortest ways to get to those targeted destination. Apparently, they travel in specific roots zigzagging to cover particular villages or landmarks of significance perhaps due to social, religious and political reasons.

As stated elsewhere, scholars have discovered that there are three versions of Aṣhtanārī Sandēśaya whose destinations are three different places. Sannasgala (p 585) observes that one version starts from Nāthagane, travels through Mīgahakumbura and ends at Handapāngama Devala at Uyanvatta in the same Kurunegala District. The purpose of this particular version of Sandēśaya is unknown. It appears to be a short distance journey when it is searched for on the Google Map. As stated elsewhere, this version is not found and cannot be reviewed at this stage.

I have noted the version published by Appuhamy in 1909 shows that the journey starts from Nāthagane and reaches Kataragama Devala situated at Diddeniya in the same district of Kurunegala. The 22 locations described in the travel path are: Nāthagane, Mīgaskumbura, Uyanwaththa, Walpola, Kadavatkæle, Kollægala, Batupitiya, Randenivela, Yaddessākanda, Dolukanda, Dunupathānge, Vallāgala, Mudannāpola, Māguruoya, Alupothagama, Dematavæva, Balaluvāgāra, Thissawa, Yongama, Sērugolla, Dæduru Oya, Diwulvæva, and Diddeniya Devala. The duty of the eight women was to hand over the Sandēśaya to Kataragama Devala at Diddeniya.

The topographical observations show that there are villages located along the route at short distances up to Diwulvæva. No villages have been described for nearly 15 to 20 Kilometres along the way until Diddeniya. It seems that this version is short of some stanzas. Appuhāmi's publication and Sinhala Vishwakōshaya identify 76 stanzas in this poem. I believe that some stanzas describing the villages from Diwulvæva to Diddeniya could have gone missing, or the poet could have lost interest in describing the villages along the way in that distance, or the poet might have found them of less significance to describe in the distance between Diwulvæva and Diddeniya.

The path taken in the full version of Aṣhtanārī Sandēśaya (as of LB, M1 and M2) starts from Nāthagane and ends at Gaṭulāgan Vihāre in Anuradhapura District.

This version also takes the same path covering the same villages and places of significance up to Diwulvæva. Afterwards 57 more locations have been described up to Gaṭulāgan vihara. I have added five newly found villages from Pohoravatta version (PV) and one from A1 version increasing the total number of landmarks up to 85 – in this way, the present publication of Aṣhtanārī Sandēśaya covers all locations spreading over 131 stanzas.

Accordingly, the full list of the places and the villages include Nāthagane (verse 16), Mīgaskumbura (verse 19), Uyanwaththa (verse 20), Walpola (verse 21), Kadawathakælē (verse 22), Kollægala (verse 23), Batupitigama (verse 26), Randenivela (verse 27), Yaddessākanda (verse 29), Dolukanda (verse 31), Dunupatăṅge (verse 33), Wallāgala (verse 34), Mudannāpola (verse 38), Vællāgala (verse 40), Māguruoya (verse 43), Alupothāgama (verse 44), Wilgam Demata Væva (verse 48), Balaluvāgāra (verse 49), Thissō Vela (verse 50), Yongama (verse 51), Sērugolla (verse 52), Nuvara Kanda (verse 54) Dæduru Oya (verse 56), Nindagama (verse 59), Diwulvæva (verse 61), Kimbulvāna Oya (verse 65), Handapāngama (verse 66), Kiralā Gedara (verse 67), Palugassæva (verse 68), Moragasvæva (verse 69), Matiyakgama (verse 70), Nāgolla (verse 71), Karambē Pidivilla (verse 72), Dahanagama (verse 73), Niyadavanē Vihāre (verse 74), Pothuvæl Pitiya (verse 75), Thalpathgiri Kanda (verse 76), Pāmihan Kanda (verse 77), Yāpahu Gam Giriya (verse 78), Kattambu Gam Giraya (verse 79), Mūnamola (verse 80), Ambagasvæva (verse 81), Mī Oya (verse 81), Nāpā Ella (verse 82), ūrāpola (verse 83), Rambāvæva (verse 84), Dematagampitiya (verse 85), Galgiriyā Kanda (verse 86), Galgiriyā Væva (verse 87), Boravæva (verse 88), Thalāṅda Pitiya (verse 89), Siyambalangamuva (verse 90), Habara Vahtta (verse 91), Kandulugamuva (verse 92), Kallanchiya (verse 93), Nēgama (verse 94), Niyangama (verse 96), Walasvæva (verse 97), Awukana vihara (verse 98), Kalā Oya (verse 99), Puliyan Kulama (verse 100), Mayilan Perumāwa (verse 101), Mudaperumā Gama (verse 102), Ihalagama (verse 103), Kāgama (verse 103), Rathnāgala (verse 104), Halmilla Væva (verse 104), Etawīravæva (verse 106), Nochchikulama (verse 107), Thōruvæva (verse 108), Kaduruvægama (verse 109), Maminiyāwa (verse 110), Ambathale Vela (verse 111), Ritigala Kanda (verse 112), Ambatale (verse 113), Kananpediyāgama (verse 114), Thōran Kulama (verse 115), Kattamurichchāna (verse 116), Sondavila (verse 117), Ulagalla Væva (verse 118), Ulagalla (verse 119), Mārā Kulama (verse 123), Utti Maduva (verse 124), Orukkumān Kulama (verse 125), and Gaṭulāgan Vihāre (verse 128).

In terms of geographical significance, Samanola Kanda (Adams Peak - distantly seen from the path), Dolu Kanda, Yaddessākanda, Galgiriya Kanda, Māguru Oya, Dǣduru Oya, Mi Oya, Kala Oya, Riṭigala Kanda are significant landmarks on the path. In addition, there are names of a number of man-made water reservoirs (Vǣva) and extensive paddy lands. Yāpahuwa is a rock where an old capital city was located. Adams Peak, Niyadawane Vihāre, Awukana and Gaṭulāgan Vihāre are renowned Buddhist shrines along the path.

Recognising the villages with South Indian legacy

I believe that some main villages along this zigzagging travel path have a significant character.

I present the theory that those villages are the places where many prominent South Indian migrants were settled and land awards, authoritative names and titles were given to them during the Kotte period (Bandaranayake 2021). Those migrants were absorbed into Sinhala Buddhist community. Nārisath Sandēśaya refers to a sword held Mudali of Uduveriya - Uduveriya Bandara (Nārisath Sandēśaya stanza 77). He was a Malala prince who came to Sri Lanka during the time of Mundukondapola Kingdom and was awarded Uduveriya, a large division or Vanni Rata or Vanni Hathpattuwa to be in charge (Bandaranayake 2021). He was regarded as an aggressive chieftain who ruled the region by the sword. He is supposed to be a prominent warrior chief of the king's army and therefore, he earned the kings patience (Bandaranayake, 2021). It is inevitable that the poet had the responsibility to acknowledge the rata (territory) that belonged to this famous chieftain. It was on the way to Dambulla Vihāre.

Nikawāgampaha Brāhmanavaliya[34] manuscript provides details about a group of Brāhmi chieftains who settled in Nikawāgampaha

---

[34] This manuscript gives details about seven Brāhmin families who came to Sri Lanka during Mundukondapola Kingdom and settled down in seven villages

Kōrale. Among the villages and divisions where they were settled include Dematagam Pitiya (Dembatogama), Rakvāna, Rambewa, Galgiriyawa, Borawewa, Thalāňda Pitiya etc. These villages on the route have been particularly celebrated . Did the poet have any allegiance to these villages and their chieftains? Nikawāgampaha Brāhmanavaliya mentions about a drummer family (Nakathi caste) who was accompanied by Dembatogama Purohit Brahmana Rāla. This drummer was settled at Valpāluva village next to the Purohits residence at Dembatogama (Bandaranayake, 2021, p 17).

Vitti manuscripts provide details about various professional groups who came to Sri Lanka and settled in Sath Kōrale together with the migrant groups of Brāhmins, Malala Princesses and Hettis (Bandaranayake 2021, page 127-133, Obeyesekere, 2005). The author could have been a descendent of Hindu servicemen who came to serve the kings of Mundukondapola and chieftains of Sath Kōrale. Or they were the companions of South Indian Brāhmi Purohits for the purpose of carrying out Hindu services and rituals (Bandaranayake, 2021, p16-19).

Srilak Kadayuru manuscript counts 100s of Brāhmi villages in Mundukondapola kingdom alone (Obeyesekere, 2005, p68, Bandaranayake 2021). Kurunegala Vistharaya manuscript lists 500 houses of Brāhmins in Kurunegala city alone (Kuruwita, 2015; Bandaranayake, 2022, page 158).

As already mentioned elsewhere, Ulagalla Disāwa and his clan were descendants of a South Indian prince. Therefore, the author who appeared to be associated with local chieftains of Sath Kōrale, had some allegiance to them, and recognised them in his poem. He then goes to recognise the descendants of South Indian origin in Nuwarakalāwiya and fulfil the duty and allegiance to Ulagalla Disāwa.

---

including the details of land grants and authoritative titles given to them (Bandaranayake, 2021, 2022).

The South Indian migrants were absorbed into Sinhala community and converted into Buddhism within a short period of time (Bandaranayake, 2021). Aṣhtanārī Sandēśaya can be a fine reflection on the Sinhala Buddhist community with South Indian origin and a celebration of their network.

Layout of the pageant

We have the question that weather the journey that described in Aṣhtanārī Sandēśaya was a reality.

Meghadūta and many other bird messenger poems were layout of imaginative and inventive masterpieces. However, Nārisath and Aṣhtanārī Sandēśaya could have been a small or large scale real events of travel. The last verse of the Nārisath Sandēśaya says that the journey took seven days; it is understood that the party walked slowly and stayed overnight at some places. It is clear that the party consisted of young women. They all needed attendants, accommodation and food along the way. The poet apparently composed the Nārisath Sandēśaya at the request made by the seven women after return from their visit to Dambulla Vihāre (Nārisath Sandēśaya verse 143-144). This explains that they have enjoyed the spectacle of the journey and wanted to relive in their memory.

Aṣhtanārī Sandēśaya and Nārisath Sandēśaya poets may have thought about making these journeys more festive and celebrative. Ulagalla cause was centred around a high-ranking chieftain, a Disāwa, who enjoyed the local political power and privileges. For example, Andirishāmi (1909, p5) believes that the parade contains many men and women. Nārisath Sandēśaya stanza 20 explains that the men who walked in the front section carried swords. Carrying a sword in a journey sounds strange. However, it cannot be for spiritual reasons.

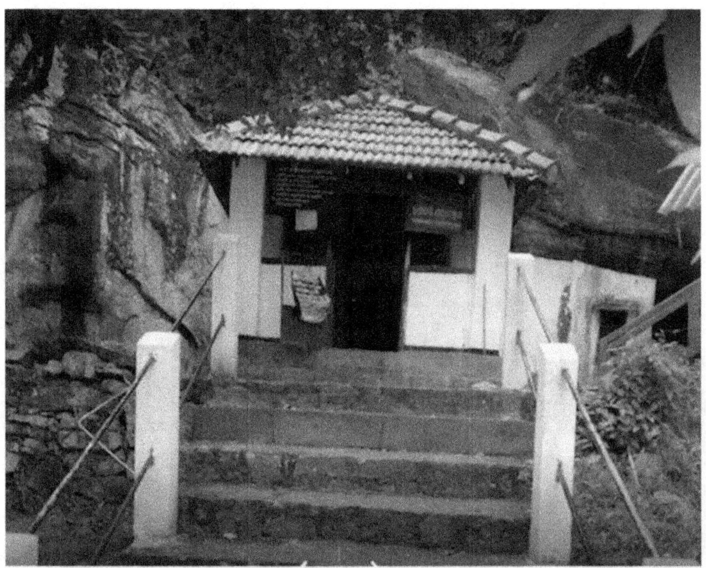

Picture 1: Nāthagane Pattini Devala (current)

It appears that the travel party of Aṣhtanārī Sandēśaya comprised many participants, i.e. sward bearers, flag bearers, drummers, attendants, and entourage. The verse 17 states the way the parade of young women left Nāthagane with jubilation and a large group of people assembled there to wish them well, "රොක්උනු සෙන් සමඟ යනමං සිනාවේ". The verse 61 states that "දවුල් බෙර මොරහු පෙරටුව යන කළ මා" which interprets that the procession was headed by drummers. There could have been other professionals and artists like dancers who joined the pageant. They all needed sponsorship for accommodation and food along the way. The local chieftains could have welcomed the party at each village and looked after their welfare. That could have been the reason for the party to take a meandering route to cover prominent villages and sponsors.

The pageant actually took place in "Bak masa" (verse 1), the celebrative month of April. Hindu and Sinhala new year celebrations take place in Bak masa (April) after the Maha harvest of rice (September to April) in Sath Kōrale and Nuvarakalāviya. It was ideal to launch the Sandēśaya pageant during this time. As it was the festive season a large number of people could have participated in the pageant. The eight young women were followed by a group of drummers, potentially from the author's clan. The leading young women dressed in a special costume bearing the Sandēśaya could have enjoyed some high position.

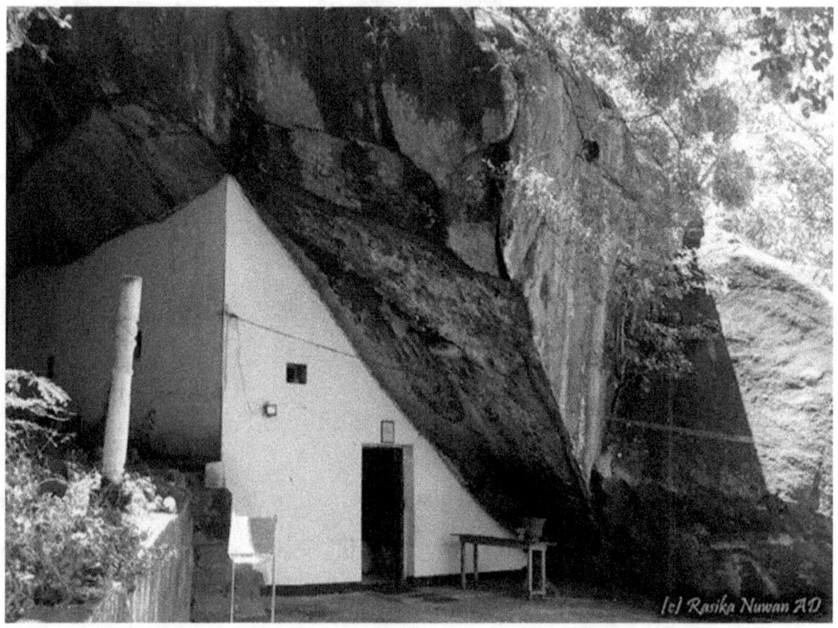

Picture 2: Gatulāgan Vihāra Worship Chamber

The journey was not something done in a hurry but took some time to absorb the festivity. The participation of pretty and elegantly dressed eight young women added to the spectacle. This was a gala event for the region and the chieftains along the path received the traveling party with honour. Moreover, the local chieftains were fully aware of the purpose and therefore, they were supportive of Ulagalla cause. It was also an event that provided people with opportunity to celebrate family connections.

It appears that there is a mysterious story behind Aṣhtanārī Sandēśaya . We will never be able to know it with certainty. But I tend to present the theory that Aṣhtanārī Sandēśaya reflects an underlined and hidden story of solidarity among Sinhala Buddhist chieftains and professionals with South Indian origin in Sath Kōrale and Nuvarakalāviya.

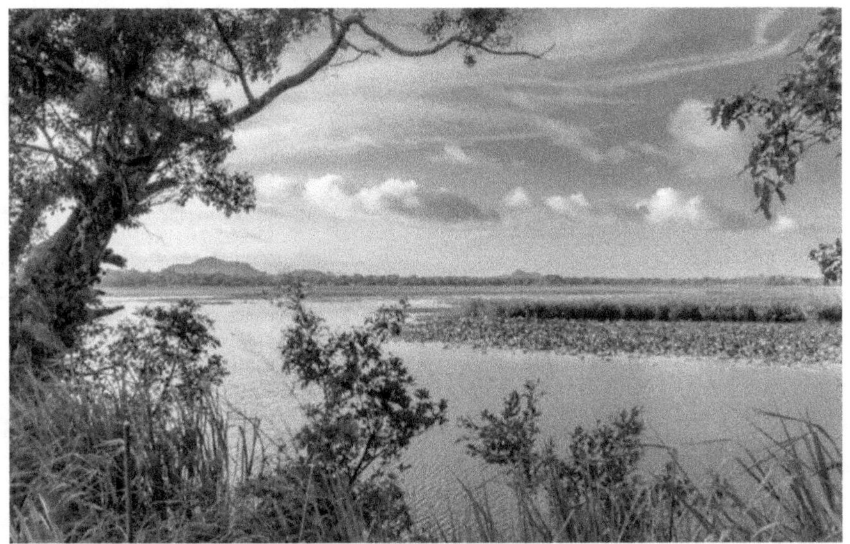

Picture 3: Ulagalla Reservoir

Another important dimension is the literary value of this Sandēśaya. After all, it was a Kāvya supposed to be read or heard by a wider audience. I would like to dedicate the next chapter to summarise the poetic narration of the Sandēśaya and appraise its literary value very briefly before presenting the poems.

Chapter 7:

Aṣhtanārī Sandēśaya - Literary Appreciation

This chapter presents a literary appreciation of Aṣhtanārī Sandēśaya for the benefit of the reader to understand its scope and its place in Sinhala Kāvya literature.

A succinct comparison was made with Salalihini Sandēśaya, the apex of the classical Sinhala Sandēśaya, to show where Aṣhtanārī Sandēśaya stands among more advanced poetic creations.

Salalihini Sandēśaya was sent to God Vibhishana at Kalani Raja Maha Vihara invoking him to bless Ulakudaya Devi, a daughter of King Parakramabahu VI (1412-1469 AD), with a son. As Salalihini Sandēśaya, written by Venerable Thotagamuwē Sri Rāhula (1410 to 1480 AD) the scholarly master of Sinhala poetry, is beyond compare care should be taken so as not to do an injustice to the humble layman poet at Mæṭioḷuva.

Challenge faced by the poet of Aṣhtanārī Sandēśaya

We have to assume that Aṣhtanārī Sandēśaya has been written as a response to an invitation. Therefore, it can be a task assigned to a poet by a sponsor who was aware of the competence of the poet to complete the task. It would certainly be more beneficial if the poet had known the sponsor (beneficiary) closely.

The poet should have had a good comprehension of the subject matter, devotion, and an intimate involvement in it. In the absence of any of the above, the poetic creativity and sentiment would be largely affected resulting in an artificial work. Furthermore, the author should have participated in the pageant, experienced the sentiment, and generated creative ideas for the poems while being involved in it.

The occasion of reciting the poems finally to an audience could have been a colourful ceremony or a gathering to celebrate the grand accomplishment.

The imagery and auditory nature of Aṣhtanārī Sandēśaya

Poetry or Kāvya is an auditory medium through which feelings and ideas are generated on a subject by using distinctive styles and rhythmic abilities of a language. Kāvyas are generally supposed to be read and heard by others to evoke vivid imaginations, feelings and meanings. In other words, Kāvya is meant to be heard, seen by the mental images, and interpreted by mind.

What does Aṣhtanārī Sandēśaya depict for a listener or a reader? The title of the poem indicates what is the poem is all about and lays a foundation for the imagery and feelings.

The first impression of this Sandēśaya is an illusory image of eight stunning young women and their involvement in delivering a manuscript containing a righteous message. The audience with a good knowledge of classical Sandēśa Kāvya could not have had any difficulty to understand the structure and the relevant segments. Those who are not familiar with the classical Sandēśa model obviously would depend on the poet's ability to induce a taste in them with his language skills.

Structure of Aṣhtanārī Sandēśaya

The initial version of Aṣhtanārī Sandēśaya has 108 stanzas (as in BL, M1, M2) whereas this extended version presents 131 stanzas with the addition of new poems from different versions. Briefly, the structure of Aṣhtanārī Sandēśaya can be identified under six sections:

1. **Introduction to the poet and launching the Sandēśaya** (verses 1-4): This section reveals the eminence of the poet as proclaimed by himself and the location of his residence, the time period of the year in which the Sandēśaya was inaugurated, and the invitation to readers/listeners to enjoy the remaining verses of this poem.

2. **Praise of the messengers – Dūta warnanā - ** (verses 5 to 17): This section provides an elaborative praise of the elegance of the eight damsels. The poet uses a figurative language in abundance referring to their stature, faces, eyes, breasts, hair, dresses, walk, ornaments, cosmetics, smile etc. In addition, the way the spectators were standing by the way side to catch the sight of the parading women, and how animals were duped into misconception by the elegant features of the young women have been profusely applauded.

3. **Praising the landmarks on the route - Mārga warnanā** (verses 18 to 117 and 123 to 125): The stanzas in this section refer to nearly 80 landmarks on the route to Gaṭulāgan Vihāre. There is not much description of most of the landmarks and their surroundings but the beauty of the eight damsels at each of the landmark repeatedly described.

4. **Praising the inheritance of Ulagalla (the beneficiary)** (verses 118 to 122): This section gives an image of the Ulagalla's legacy he inherited from his ancestor Ilangasinghe Kalu Kumara. The

Ulagalla reservoir and its scenery, extensive land, vegetation, and gardens are elegantly portrayed. Ulagalla mansion and its extensive amenities consisting of store houses of grains (barns), guard houses, strong droves of elephants, horses and travel carts are pronounced. Royal awards of lands and honorary titles conferred upon Ulagalla ancestry are graciously reminded.

5. **Veneration of Gaṭulāgan Vihāre (the destination)** (verses 126 to 129): The Gaṭulāgan Vihāre is a sacred place of Buddhists visited by myriads of devotees, consisting of bright façades, stylish carpets, artistic ivory carvings and blue flags fluttering over the fence of burning votive lamps (made of clay). The poet encourages the damsels to worship at this sacred place with the utmost devotion and respect.

6. **Presenting the Sandēśaya (the message)** (130 to 131). This section describes the message the poem contains. It is a respectful plea made to the deities at Gaṭulāgan Vihāre complex to help to recover the lost land and territories awarded to the ancestors of Ulagalla disawa by the great King Buvanekabahu. It also carries an appeal to bring well wishes for Ulagalla Disawa.

Every poem consists of four lines. The poet has taken a meticulous care for consistent lineation, feet and rhyme pattern of each verse.

Structural comparison with Classical Sandēśa

All classical Sandēśa such as Salalihini, Mayura, Thisara, Paravi, Kōkila, Girā and Hansa have a set structure. They start with a warm welcome to the dūta followed by the praise of dūta; mention of the recipient of the message; acclamation of the departure from the city and the ruler of the city; instructions given to the Duta to carry out the duty, itinerary and connected details, and explanation of the message with relevant details, and final blessings on dūta.

As already noted above, Aṣhtanārī Sandēśaya deviates from the classical Sandēśa model (structure). Aṣhtanārī Sandēśaya starts with the praise of the poet himself. Aṣhtanārī Sandēśaya lacks welcome the dūta, ten-line stanza form known as "Dasapada Hælla", and the concluding segment of blessings on dūta.

Salalihini Sandēśaya has been created in such a way that its mission would not fail. As stated elsewhere, the intention of Salalihini Sandēśaya was to bless Ulakudaya Devi with a son, and it was subsequently fulfilled. The clarity of the message, the clarity of each role to be played in the mission, the flow, the congruence of each part in the entire poem have been meticulously maintained. In addition to the customary submission to the god Vibhishana, the poet acknowledges and seeks additional assistance from his wife and son (Verse 106 and 107) for the fulfilment of his pledge without any failure (Besides, Ulakudaya Devi was the half-sister of Venerable Totagamuvē Sri Rāhula, the poet). It is not fair to expect such an intimacy to subject matter, clarity, and craftsmanship from the poet of Aṣhtanārī Sandēśaya. The congruence of each part and the flow of conceptions and imagery are rather weak in Aṣhtanārī Sandēśaya.

In Aṣhtanārī Sandēśaya there are 108 stanzas (according to the original form of BL, M1 and M2) as in Salalihini Sandēśaya. The poet wishes to get his work admired and keep in parallel to the size of the masterpiece (Salalihini Sandēśaya).

Point of view

The point of view puts the reader or the listener inside the fictional world of the poet. Mostly the second and third person points of view have been employed by the poet in Aṣhtanārī Sandēśaya. The first part of the Sandēśaya is written in the first and third person points of view. The second part which illuminates the beauty and elegance of the young women (dūta) has been written in the third person using graphic descriptions to build the image of the damsels. The third part, the praising of the landmarks (Mārga warnanā) is written in the second and third person points of view, like giving travel directions and visual commentary to the damsels about the localities that they pass. The rhyme scheme has been maintained so that the name of the landmark is rhymed with the end word of each line.

As stated elsewhere, the repetition of similes and metaphors to describe the damsels at each landmark has been a hindrance to the reader who focuses on the entire Sandēśaya. However, I find that many villagers along the actual path of this Sandēśaya have committed into the memory the stanzas that described their localities. Those stanzas were memorable because of their association with such illusory and elegant eight damsels. The Sandēśa poetry could not have been a novelty for these villagers. However, I have found that they were not aware of all the verses of Aṣhtanārī Sandēśaya. I became interested in this Sandēśaya in my late adolescence because it describes a few landmarks in my home area. As I had no access to the full version, I was not aware of the purpose of the Sandēśaya at all.

The last two sections of this Sandēśaya have been composed in the second person point of view. For the entire poetry mostly the second and third person points of view have been used in the entire poem.

In contrast, Salalihini Sandēśaya and all other classical Sinhala Sandēśas have been written consistently from the second person point of view while directly addressing and guiding the dūta. That manner provides a rich sensory experience for the listener to be close with the dūta during the entire journey. The mix of first, second and third person points of view in Aṣhtanārī Sandēśaya slightly interfered with the sensory experience of its listeners.

Mood and Tone

The mood is how the author wants the reader to feel, when someone reads or listens to his/her work. It is communicated subtly through images starting with stimuli, causing emotions and creating feelings. This mood concept coincides with Indian classical poetical concept of "rasa". The tone is how the author himself/herself feels about their subject matter. The tone will often be closely related to the mood of the piece of poetry.

There are two moods found in Aṣhtanārī Sandēśaya, i.e. the desirability of sensual beauty ("sringāra rasa" - erotism and natural beauty) and the promoting of spirituality ("bhakti" - religious reverence and devotion). The spirituality coincides with the classical Indian rasa Kārunyam (compassion or mercy) and with the rasa shāntham (peace and tranquillity) (Manamohan 2002). These two contrasting moods (sringāra and spirituality) make Aṣhtanārī Sandēśaya more appealing. Both moods are predictable considering the selection of eight young women (damsels) as messengers, the empathetic purpose and intention of the Sandēśaya.

Sringāra rasa can be generated in poetry by words, erotic image, attire, and action. In Aṣhtanārī Sandēśaya, the sringāra rasa is particularly expressed in the verses from 5 to 17 where the image of beauty is portrayed. Further the sringāra rasa is repeatedly promoted by praising their modest beauty and erotic presence at each landmark throughout the journey.

Sringāra rasa gives scope for a multitude of emotions. For example, this term in Sanskrit is interpreted as natural beauty, decoration, attractiveness and aesthetic sense. Therefore, sringāra rasa emerges in the praise of natural beauty and imagery of the landmarks. A few examples of sringāra rasa generated in Aṣhtanārī Sandēśaya are provided under the forthcoming heading figure of speech.

The mood of spirituality (rasas of Kārunyam and shāntham) sprouts from the admiring and acknowledging all the places of worship of Buddhists and god's shrines (vihara and devāla). This is also found in the invitation to worship at the sacred places to achieve spirituality. For example, the journey starts reminding the damsels to glance at Mount Srī Pāda (Adams Peak) towards south, whare the Buddha is believed to have set his foot print (verse 18). The poet has copied this ritual from the Salalihini Sandēśaya in which the dūta is asked to behold the Adams Peak located towards the east (Salalihini Sandēśaya stanza 25, "sakisaṅda penē samanola gala nægenahira"). Among the Buddhist shrines, the damsels are urged to worship on their way include Kollægala vihara (verses 23 to 25), sacred Dolu Kanda (verses 31 and 32), Vallāgala Vihara (verses 34 to 36), Niyadavane vihara (verse 74), Awukana Vihara (verse 98) and finally Gaṭulāgan Vihara (128 and 129). The poem devoted to Gaṭulāgan vihara (verse 129) is a fine example of the spirituality taught in Buddhism:

සෙනා දිදී එන සෙනගන් නොඔා ඇ   දු
පිනා සසර සාගරයන් ගෙවා යෙ   දු
නානා මේ යුදයදී මුදුනත් තබා ඉ   දු
නුනා පැලදි සළු මුදුනත් තබා ව   දු

The damsels are asked to join the throng who worship at the sacred place and swim across the ocean of existence (reach the end of existence).

I believe that the mood of Salalihini Sandēśaya is primarily represented by the blend of four elements of rasa vīryam (heroism), shāntham (peace and tranquillity), kāruṇyam (compassion and mercy) and sringāra (erotic love). Not only Salalihini Sandēśaya but also Girā, Paravi and Kokila Sandēśa praise the heroism of the King Parakramabahu VI who unified Sri Lanka and created an atmosphere for prosperity (Salalihini Sandēśaya verses 18 to 20). The capital city of Jayewardenepura from where he reigned the country is eulogised highly (verses 7 to 14) along with the city of Kelaniya (verses 53 to 58). Spirituality is demonstrated by repeatedly asking the dūta to worship at Kelani vihara (verses 59 to 71) and fondly praising the power and glory of God Vibhishana (verses 77 to 92). Peace and tranquillity are vividly depicted throughout Salalihini Sandēśaya, whereas Aṣhtanārī Sandēśaya lacks that merit.

Tone and attitude

I think the tone of Aṣhtanārī Sandēśaya is friendly, pleasant and optimistic. It helps to enhance the emotions of the reader/listener. The splendour of the damsels is imaginative and inviting and the sceneries on either side of the route of the procession is impressive. The poet takes the reader through a journey with heightened calmness and composure.

The poet mostly addresses the damsels with respect and gratitude. Among the terms used in BL, M1, and M2 versions to refer to the damsels include the words "liya", "laňda", "laňdagano", "mithura", and "næna" which are warm, admirable and adorable forms of address. However, there is a change of the way the damsels were addressed and demanded to perform certain actions; particularly in A1 version include "yava", "yavu", "karanev" and "thopi" which sound less courteous. It seems that the poet, who introduces several new poems to A1 has a different attitude towards the damsels, and he displays a lesser academic discipline.

The respectful tone of the Salalihini Sandēśaya is maintained throughout the poetry addressing the dūta (Salalihini bird) as if a friend (mithura) of high caste is addressed.

Figures of speech in Aṣhtanārī Sandēśaya

The figures of speech are defined as giving different meanings to objects and events instead of their literal meaning. Figurative language makes an idea or an image more interesting and exciting. The use of figures of speech allows the reader to experience unforeseen comparisons and encounter curious word conventions. Figures of speech also help to illuminate what a writer wants to convey creatively.

Figures of speech include metaphors, similes, hyperboles and personifications which paint images beyond the obvious. They also appeal to readers' senses, preconceived notions, contextual inferences, and connections.

Similes (upamā) and Metaphors (upamā rupaka)

What are the highlights of figures of speech in Aṣhtanārī Sandēśaya?

Metaphors and similes are used to make comparisons of two things. A simile compares two things using the words "like" or "as". A metaphor makes comparisons without using "like" or "as". A hyperbole is a figure of speech that exaggerates ideas and concepts.

Metaphors, similes and hyperboles are found in abundance in Aṣhtanārī Sandēśaya. The following are notable examples of similes and metaphors that generate eroticism (sringāra rasa) with vivid imagery.

- සබඳ මුව තඹර සඳකැළුමෙකි සෝබන - sabanda muwa thaṁbara saňda kælumeki sobana (Verse 7). The faces of young women are compared to lotus flowers and the enchanting moonlight.

- ලැමෙද දිළි දෙකුඹු විදුලිය වෙති කොටන - læmeda dili dekuṁbu viduliya vethi kotana (verse 7). The full breasts (resembling a pair of round pots) are compared to lightening.

- බිඹුපල කියා දෙතොලට රැවටී රණ ගිරා - bimbupala kiyā detholata rævati rana girā (verse 11). Their full lips are compared to ripe fruit (parrots get deceived by the full lips that resemble ripe fruit).

- මැනික් කියා රැවටුනි උරඟු දෙනෙතට - mænik kiyā rævatuni uraňgu denethata (verse 12). Eyes are compared to gems (cobras are confused at the sight of the eyes glimmering like gems).

- රැවටුනු විධ දණෝ තම සුරඹ ලිය කියා - Rævatunu vidha daṇō tama suramba liya kiyā (verse 13). Eight women are compared to goddesses (Men are deceived by the sight of the women looking like goddesses)

- ලිහිණිය රවටුනා වෙනි තන මඩල දැක - lihiniya rǣvatunā veni tana madala dǣka (verse 14). Their breasts are compared to lihiniya birds (lihiniyas are deceived by the sight of breasts mistaking them for two of their kind)

- නිල් වරලෙසට රවටුනු කින්ද බකමූනු - nil varalesata rǣvatunu kinda bakamūnu (verse 15). The colour of hair (of the women) is compared to that of owls feather (owls are confused at the sight of their black hair)

- නිල් මේකුලෙව් වරලස උනමින් දිගට - nil mekulevu varalasa unamin digata (verse 46). Their cascading black hair is compared to a rain cloud.

Salalihini Sandēśaya is renowned for similes and metaphors.

- බිතු සිතුවම් රූ මෙන් පිටු නොපා විති (verse 4). Friends are always there like frescoes that do not turn back either at sadness or happiness

- රැඳි රළ රළැති හොයා දියවන්නා නමැති ඇඳිපුර අඟන පට සළු සිරි දපැයි තිනි (verse 8). The quietly flowing Diyawanna Oya across the city of Jayawardanapura look like an attire of a pretty woman.

- තර කළ විසල් වාසල් යතුරු මෙනුවරල බැඳ හළ රුවන් තන පට කියෙලිය පවුර (verse 9). The wall around the city of Jayawardanapura resembles a gem-studded brassiere a young woman is wearing.

- සිරිමත් සුපුන් සඳ වැනි දුවන මනහර (verse 64). Attractive face is like the beautiful full moon.

All these examples from both Sandēśaya are hyperboles where the reality is exaggerated.

Sringāra rasa

There are ample examples where sringāra rasa has been elicited referring to the way the damsels were appealing erotically to young men in Aṣhtanārī Sandēśaya.

Verse 46 is a generous example:

නිල මෙකුලෙව් වරලස උනමින් දිග ට

අල්මේ සිතින් සලෙලුන් දෙස විටින් වි ට

බැලුන් ලමින් සිටි ඒ වරගණන් හ ට

බැලුම් එවොත් බඔසරවත් කැදෙයි දු ට

The noble young women with cascading hair, that resembles a rain cloud, glance at the young men from time to time, if their glances are returned even the celibacy of young men will be broken.

The following verse (95) shows that the poet has some bias to praise the beauty of Moor (Muslim) women in rice fields and markets in Nēgama village (verses 94 and 95) .

දුල් පුල් මල් පියුම් පෙති බඳ මුතු බහ ණා

මල් තැලි දෙකුඹු මුතු ගෝබර පෙති සේ ණා

නිල් පුල් මල් දෙනෙත් බැම තුරු යුග පා ණා

සල් පිල් වල සිටිණ යොන් ලිය අසමා ණා

The young Muslim women with eyes like blue lilies, wearing gorgeous jewellery, are of incomparable exquisite beauty.

Salalihini Sandēśaya is renowned for the elegance of its sringāra rasa. The verse (13) referring to the women at Jayavardanepura elicits an image of their splendid beauty.

සිසි වන වුවන ඉඟසුග ගත හැකි මිටි න

නිසි පුඑලුලුකුල රිය සක යුරු තිසර ත න

දිසි රණ ලියෙව් රැසිරි යුත් මෙ පුරඟ න

ඇසි පිය හෙළන පමණින් නොවෙති දෙවඟ න

Further describing the women dancing at the royal palace, the author creates a memorable image of their splendour, attire, and appearance (verse 74).

විදෙන ලෙළෙන තරුබර පුළුකුළ රැ   ද

හෙළන නගන අත නුවනග බැලුම් දි   ද

රුවින දිලෙන අබරණ කැලුම ගත යේ   ද

සැලෙන පහන සිළු වැනි රඟන ලිය සැ   ද

The verse (47) creates an image of the women at bath in Kelani river.

නුවතින් නිල උපුල් මද හසිනි හෙළැඹු   ල

වුවතින් කමල් පෑ ලවනතිනි රතු පු   ල

පවතින් අඹල රත ලිය වන් ලියන් කැ   ල

රුවතින් ලකළ ගඟ දිය කෙල නුමුණු ක   ල

The eyes of the women have been compared to blue lilies, pleasant smile to white lilies, the faces to lotus, lips to red lilies, and all the women are compared to golden vines that flutter in the gentle wind. The poet cleverly paints an exquisite image in the listener's mind. Some of these similes and metaphors have been copied by Aṣhtanārī Sandēśaya.

Glimpses of Dūta warnanā in Aṣhtanārī Sandēśaya

Aṣhtanārī Sandēśaya is full of high praise of the bevy of eight young women who carries the message. I would like to pick dūta warnanā particularly for an appreciation. It appears that the eight messenger girls win high praise from the poet for their elegant figures, the fascinating smile, impressive gait, ornamental attire, and glittering ornaments.

Corporeal elegance of the feminine figure is highly praised so as to keep the readers enchanted. The poet creates an image in the mind of readers comparing their face to the full moon (punsanda පුන්සඳ - verse 8), and at some other occasion to lotus in full bloom (muva thaṁbara මුව තඹර - verse 102 and rataṁbara pethi muva රත්තඹර පෙති මුව –

verse 59). At several occasions the poet admires how their tresses of black hair has been decorated with flowers (diṅgu varala bæňdi mal rēnu yomā - දිඟු වරල බැඳි මල් රේණු යොමා - verse 22, nillā diṅgu varala bændi mal koňda sodura නිල්ලා දිඟු වරල බැඳි මල් කොඳ සොදුර - verse 23, and පිරා නිල් වරල බැඳිමල් සේ සොඹණ - verse 83). Their forehead compared to the crescent (adasanda paṭu nalala aḍa saňda verse 73). Their eyes are compared to blue safire (ratu nila miṇi denata රතු නිල මිණි දෙනත, verse 6 and nilpulmal denet නිල් පුල් මල් දෙනෙත් - verse 95). Their teeth are compared to glittering pearls (mutu dala depela මුතු දල දෙපෙළ දිළි - verse 6) and their neck is that of a peacock (sikinidu gela සිකිනිදු ගෙල verse 11; sikinidu vara bella සිකිනිදු වර බෙල්ල verse 82; sikhinidu kara සිකිනිදු කර verse 70). Breasts look like full and round pots (kumˇbu læmæda කුඹු ලැමැද – verse 106), and they have been created by the supreme god (kumˇbā piyayuru bamˇbā amˇbuwa කුඹා පියයුරු බඹා ඇඹුව – verse 42), lips are like ripe fruits that arouse sensual feelings (බිඹුපල කියා දෙතොලට - verse 11).

They walk impressively in the manner of a majestic tusker (sakmaṇa gamaṇa kumˇbu lela dena thumāgē සක්මණ ගමණ කුඹු ලෙල දෙන තුමාගේ - verse 5) and they smile charmingly. They appear to be wearing glittering jewellery and pearls of purity; they drape expensive silk cloths (kasun vath hæňḍa særasī sobaṇa කසුන් වත් හැඳ සැරසී සොඹණ - verse 16) around their thin waist looking like a bow[35] (thin long curved piece of wood of which a bow is made) (ran rada dunu miteka thuṇu iṅgalā saḷuwa රන් රද දුනු මිටෙක තුණු ඉඟලා සළුව - verse 8).

The spectators along the way are captivated by the spectacle of messenger girls of exquisite beauty.

---

[35] Thin long curved piece of wood of which a bow is made.

Rhythm

Rhythm is an audible pattern or effect created by introducing pauses or stress on certain words in the poem. Aṣhtanārī Sandēśaya has used rhythms in abundance and harmoniously. The verses 4, 20, 35, 39, 50, and 119 are a few of noteworthy examples. In particular, I would like to draw attention to verses 35, 39 and 119, where remarkable rhythms are printed bold (initial rhymes, internal rhymes and end rhymes). They provide ample linguistic patterns and sounds which give the poems a musical effect (melody):

නිල්ලා වත සොම්පුල්ලා ලඳ ලැම තුල තැල්	ල
තෙල්ලා ඉස පැටලිල්ලා වරලෙස ගැවසිල්	ල
නිල්ලා වත රළි අල්ලා රණ හන්ෂ නැවිල්	ල
වැල්ලා ගල දැක පල්ලා මිතුරේ පුරණල්	ල
රල්ලලා සළුව සිහිනිඟට තිල්ල	ලා
තැල්ලලා බැඳපු නිල් වරල එල්ල	ලා
බෙල්ලලා එරණ් දඹ කරට තැලෙල්	ලා
සොල්ලලා කතුන් එති දෙකුඹු සොල්ල	ලා
නිල්ල ජල රල්ල පිරි සුදු නැලවිල්	ල
වැල්ල සිසි ලැල්ල රතඹර ඔළු ගොල්	ල
ලොල්ල සොමී පුල්ල ඔපලඳ කොඳ නිල්	ල
දුල්ල පුරණල්ල පරසිදු උල ගල්	ල

These examples show the poet's language expertise and diligence in composing.

Salalihini Sandēśaya is full of effortless rhythms eliciting intense meanings. The following verses are examples of them (verse 53 and 63) are:

පැහැ සරණිය මිනි පැමිණිය කොත් අග	ට
බඳ කිකිණිය දඬ ගිගිනිය විමන් ව	ට
නොව පැරණිය වන රමණිය විටින් වි	ට
සැළලිහිණිය වඳු කැලණිය පුරවර	ට

පෙර උවිඳා ගෙන ගිරිඳා සිඳු සල   ත
නැගී පැහැඳා පෙන සමුඳා සැටි දිමු   ත
මෙන උළිඳා පැහැ විහිඳා නෙ දිගු බි   ත
සැඳී වටඳා ගෙයි වඳුඳා ගැබ දිමු   ත

Personifications

Personification is a literary device that gives human characteristics to nonhuman things or inanimate objects or events. It can add life, energy, and animation to motionless objects or subjects.

Among the personification examples in Aṣhtanārī Sandēśaya include "ලකකත" (verse 2) and "ලකඟන" (verse 58), in both cases Lanka is personified as a woman, විදුලිය මුකුළ කර - verse 18), lightning is personified as capable of performing human actions (flirting), පෙති යුවළ (verse 84), which compare the two petals to a couple, නිල්ල ජල රැල්ල පිරි සුදු නැලවිල්ල (verse 119), gentle waves of Ulagalla reservoir has been personified as a baby being rocked with a lullaby in a cradle.

The poet has not used many personifications in Aṣhtanārī Sandēśaya. It is possible that he lacks the ability to use personification to add life to poetry.

Language and eras of cultural difference

As noted elsewhere, classical poetry exhibits the characteristics of high degree of poetic quality and the ability of staying long in readers' mind. Several variables may contribute in some way or other to define the classical nature of the poetry, for instance, competence of the poet, expertise demonstrated in language manipulation, and the social and cultural richness where the poetry originated. Aṣhtanārī Sandēśaya and Salalihini Sandēśaya demonstrate two different dictions representing two different eras and cultural backgrounds.

Aṣhtanārī Sandēśaya was influenced by the disadvantaged nature of these variables to maintain a high degree of capacity of staying long in readers memory. The language was manipulated with poor expertise that does not appeal to the long-lasting memory. In addition, the poem was composed within a non-sophisticated social environment and the mastery of language of the poet was not classical enough to last long.

I find that Aṣhtanārī Sandēśaya has many words and usage whose meaning is beyond comprehension of reader, because the diction seems to represent a forgone era. The survival of this Sandēśaya seems to be partly due to the selection of erotic and sensual damsels as messengers. It was copied and recopied into ola leaf manuscripts by those who were fascinated by the poem.

Skills and the background of the poet

It is evident, as already mentioned elsewhere, that the poet of the earliest version of Aṣhtanārī Sandēśaya was from Mæṭioḷuva. He had a background in drumbeating, traditional dancing, astrology, and knowledge in Sanskrit and Pali languages. He seems to be a member of the Silpādhipathi clan. The other poets who made several iterations represent the same clan or a group of people who copied or added verses with admiration to the original.

The question remains how the original poet Silpādhipathi excelled in poetic abilities and was inspired to create Sandēśa poetry. All the other classical poets seem to be associated with academic institutes like key pirivena for their education. They were under the guidance of scholastic teachers and monks. The background of venerable Sri Rāhula Thera is an example. It is unlikely that Silpādhipathi attended an academic institution as such[36]. He was a product of informal or non-formal education through which he excelled in the traditional craft of his generation and legacy. His exposure to art and craft from his legacy motivated him to search for skills in other aesthetic subjects. He could have been influenced and inspired by poets and scholars like

---

[36] It is a possibility that this poet associated scholarly monks in the region and had some inspiration.

Thotagamuwē Sri Rāhula Thera. He then could have followed and modelled himself on this great erudite figure.

As stated elsewhere, I believe that this poet who composed the original Aṣhtanārī Sandēśaya possessed expertise of classical Sinhala language, knowledge of classical literature, and poetry, and was creative. I observed some elements of his capacity to understand the subtle nature of this auditory medium in which he had to elicit images and feelings in the listeners by utilising distinctive styles and rhythmic qualities of the Sinhala language. He had essentially inherited this capacity.

We can speculate that this poet or his father or grandfather had been awarded the meritorious name Silpādhipathi by the king to recognise the enormous proficiency demonstrated and the contribution made to the Muṇḍukoṇḍapola kingdom. The award replicates the historical honours like "Sakalakalā Vallabha" (master of all classical artistic subjects). Eventually, the poet had lots of courage to claim that he was a proficient and renowned poet at that time (දැක දස දින පතල කල කිව්වර විපුල).

It is also evident that the author naturally and subliminally used the drum beats like තකඬොන් in a few verses 66 and 80 which validated his professional community background. He reflects his familiarity with Tamil language. There are some verses in Aṣhtanārī Sandēśaya which have Tamil language influence. The words like සොම්පුල්ලා (verse 35, 72 and 105) පුරණැල්ලේ (verse 113) පුරණැල්ල (verse 119), මුරුක්කු පෙරුක්කු and කරැක්කු (verse 125) are good examples. They are testifying evidence to support my theory that the poet was celebrating his ancestral south Indian origin and showing allegiance and loyalty to the other South Indian lineage in Sath Kōrale and Nuvarakalāviya.

Chapter 8:

Concluding Comments

Aṣhtanārī Sandēśaya is a little known Sandēśa Kāvya or message poetry written in the early days of the kingdom of Kandy by a poet who lived at Mæṭioḷuva village in Sath Kōrale (Kurunegala District). The purpose of this Sandēśaya was to bring good wishes to Ulagalla Disāwa and to seek blessings of deities enabling him to regain his lost lands of inheritance.

The messengers of eight young women (damsels) travelled approximately 100 Kilometres from the village Nāthagane, adjoining to the poet's village Mæṭioḷuva, to Gaṭulāgan vihara, in Anuradhapura District located close to Ulagalla's manor.

Discovery and presentation

The text of Aṣhtanārī Sandēśaya had been hidden in scattered ola-leaf manuscripts, and two partial publications without being exposed to a comprehensive academic review. I believe that this publication will become a turning point in reviewing and assembling scattered manuscripts and translating them into a credible version of the original Aṣhtanārī Sandēśaya. Therefore, it is presented to a local Sri Lankan and an international audience for appreciation and preservation.

Disadvantage to Aṣhtanārī Sandēśaya

Obviously, the scholars have not incorporated Aṣhtanārī Sandēśaya into the category of major Sandēśa claiming that it is lacking in reasonable literary quality. However, I have not found credible evidence that this version of Aṣhtanārī Sandēśaya has been fully accessed and evaluated by scholars. I have seen a great deal of comments made following third party references.

I believe that the classifying it as minor Kāvya or a pilgrimage poetry has discouraged scholars to search for hidden qualities of Kāvyas like this poetry that sprouted following the classical Kotte era. Sannasgala (1964), who labelled Aṣhtanārī Sandēśaya as a pilgrimage Kāvya, appeared to have had access to a short version of this Sandēśaya of a little literary value. He apparently had disregarded that the Sandēśaya followed a typical model of classical Sandēśaya. However, Hugh Nevill seems to have a high regard for this Sandēśaya from a historical and traditional point of view of Sri Lankan poetry. I consider that Aṣhtanārī Sandēśaya is not a pilgrimage poem.

Literary value

A literary evaluation of this Sandēśaya was made for the benefit of readers to understand its broader scope. In addition, a brief comparison of Aṣhtanārī Sandēśaya was made with Salalihini Sandēśaya to get an idea of the position this work holds among more advanced works.

I believe that the poet of Aṣhtanārī Sandēśaya possessed expertise of classical Sinhala language and the knowledge of classical Sri Lankan literature. There is no doubt that the poet had copied and imitated classical models as many poets did since Meghadūta written by Kālidāsa. It seems that Salalihini Sandēśaya had been the idol of this poet.

It is reasonable to acknowledge that the poet was a scholar who grew up in rural environment and had the background of traditional arts and crafts. It seems that he has not received any form of formal education from a higher educational institution of the time. No records are available to prove that he had access to scholarly teachers and grand masters for guidance. However, he was from the distinguished Silpādhipathi breed of Mæṭioḷuva. The poet composed this poem as a response to an invitation made by Ulagalla. In contrast, erudite Venerable Thotagamuwē Sri Rāhula Thera had inner desire and inspiration to compose Salalihini Sandēśaya with full commitment to make a royal wish come true.

After all, Aṣhtanārī Sandēśaya is a work of poetry. It is worth examining the place where this Sandēśaya stands among other poetic creations. Despite some disadvantaged background, the poet of Aṣhtanārī Sandēśaya seemed to have possessed creativity and poetic insight. Poetry or Kāvya is an auditory medium through which feelings and ideas are generated on a subject by utilising distinctive styles and rhythmic abilities of a language. Kāvyas are generally supposed to be read or heard to evoke vivid imaginations, feelings and meanings. In other words, as stated elsewhere, Kāvya is to be heard by ear, and visualised and interpreted by mind. I observed some elements of the poet's capacity to understand this subtle nature of poetry.

The poet was reasonably sophisticated, his tone was calm, composed and friendly to elicit sringāra and spiritual rasas throughout the poetry. He used a rhythmic language in verses and figures of speech such as metaphors, similes, and amplification to create distinctive emotional feelings in readers or listeners. He is not included in distinguished category of classical poets of Sinhala literature. However, he deserves some recognition.

Sociological and historical value

This publication presents a commentary on the sociological, historical, and political background of Aṣhtanārī Sandēśaya which seems to reveal a hidden historical and ancestral story line.

This Sandēśaya throws some light upon a political struggle faced by chieftains of South Indian descent in Nuvarakalāviya. It is evident that migrant families of South Indian elite which moved to Sri Lanka since the Dambadeni period (1220 to 1345 AD), made Sath Kōrale and Nuvarakalāviya their home and enjoyed privileges. Eventually they were absorbed into the Sinhala Buddhist society (Bandaranayake, 2021, 2022).This Sandēśaya gives an insight into their ongoing struggle to maintain their power and privileges while being assimilated into the local Sinhala Buddhist society.

Ulagalla Disawa represents an ancestry of South Indian origin. His ancestors had won honorary titles and chieftain positions with awards of lands and territories from the king Buvanekabahu of Dambadeni Kingdom. This Sandēśaya reveals their extensive land heritage including an elegant mansion. By the time of this Sandēśaya (early 17the century) was written, the power and privileges of this ancestry were disputed, and it was felt necessary to seek humble divine intervention for some form of restoration. It appears many chieftains in Sath Kōrale, and Nuvarakalāviya of South Indian descent expressed solidarity with the Ulagalla cause.

The Sandēśaya starts from the village of Nāthagane, the capital city of the Mundukondapola regional kingdom (Sath Kōrale) into which many families of South Indian high society flocked during the Kotte Sithawaka Kingdom seeking lands and privileges to settle

(Bandaranayake, 2021 and 2022). Aṣhtanārī Sandēśaya can be a fine reflection on the Sinhala Buddhist community of South Indian origin. It is also a celebration of their network and showing of their solidarity with an allegiance to Ulagalla.

I observed that the carrying of Sandēśaya by eight damsels was an elaborate pageant sponsored by local chieftains along the way and celebrated in the festive month of Bak (April). It was a significant and colourful event for the people in Sath Korale and Nuvarakalāviya.

However, there was no evidence found to prove that the plea of the Sandēśaya became a success.

Further research

I have completed the task of presenting this less known Sandēśaya to a broader audience. I believe that I have provided some insight into the social and political background of Aṣhtanārī Sandēśaya. I have completed a reasonably fair literary evaluation using a standard framework.

I invite readers and future researchers to receive and acknowledge Aṣhtanārī Sandēśaya and to conduct further research, analysis and literary evaluations to accommodate this massage poem.

Chapter 9:
Aṣhtanārī Sandēśaya with Manuscripts Comparison

Launching the Sandēśaya and Celebrating the poet

1

සක වස[37] බක්[38] මසිනි අව දසවක ඇතු ල

නෙකරිය කුල කමල කුජ දින ලද නිම ල

රික යස මග නැකත හෝරා නිලඟ ත ල

දැක දස දිත පතල කල[39] කිව්වර විපු ල

saka vasa bak masini ava dasavaka ætula

nekariya kula kamala kuja dina lada nimala

rika yasa maga nækata hôrā nilaǧga tala

dæka dasa dita patala kala kivivara vipula

2

විකසිත පොතසකත බලවත යුතු අන ග

වක අන දද නිමල අසුරණ දිය මත ග

ලකකත සරසවිය මිහිකත බුරිව් සග ග[40]

රැකඳෙත කිව් වරණ සවුසිය මුරු සම ග

---

[37] වසි BL වස M1, M2

[38] වක් BL, M1, M2,

[39] කළ M2

[40] මිහිකත බුරිව්සගග BL, මිහිතබුරිව්සඟග M1, මිහිතබුරිව්සඟග M2,

vikasita pota sakata balavata yutu anga
vaka ana dada nimala asuraṇa diya mataga
lakakata sarasaviya mihikata burivi saśaga
rækadeta kivi varaṇa savusiya muru samaga

3   පින්පෙත් යුත් ඉදිරිසිංහ[41] රජවර බැළ   ව[42]
මණ්මත් මෙත් සිරි නිසර බඳ සිරි සිළ   ව
පැන්පත් වරණ විතරණ යන එළ නෙළ   ව
නන්ලත් ගොත් පිහිටි සිටි රට මැටිඹළ   ව

pinpet yut idirisinha rajavara bæḷuva
manmat met siri nisara baňda sirisiḷuva
pænpat varaṇa vitaraṇa yana eḷu neḷuva
nanlat got pihiṭi siṭi raṭa mæṭioḷuva

4   ඉෂ්ටකාරි වරඟණ අඟනෝ ය   න්න
පෂ්ටචාරි කයවත ඇඳලා ඔ   නන
තුෂ්ටභාරි[43] ණොනෑවත සරසඳ වැ   න්න
අෂ්ටනාරි සන්දෙසේ කවි ඔ   න්න

iṣhṭakāri varaňgaṇa aňgaṇō yanna
paṣhṭacāri kayavata æňḍalā onna
tuṣhṭabhāri ṇonævata sarasaňḍa vænna
aṣhṭanāri sandēsē kavi onna

Praising the beauty of eight damsels (Dūta)

5   දක්ෂන[44] කතක වත් හැඳ නග[45] නගා   ගේ
රොක්වෙණ වරල බැඳි මල් කොඳ තුරා   ගේ[46]
සක්මණ ගමණ කුඹුලෙල දෙන තුමා   ගේ

---

[41]   ඉදිරිසින්භ BL, ඉදිරිසිහ M1, ඉදිරිසිංභ M2
[42]   බැළැව BL (in all 4 lines in many places), බැළව M1, M2
[43]   බාරි M1
[44]   දක්සන M1, PV
[45]   කතක වන් හැඳ නදග නගාගේ M2, කතක වන් හෙද නැත නගාගේ PV
[46]   රොක් වෙන වර බුදින කොඳ මල් තුරා ගේ PV

ලස්සන[47] කියනු බැරි ලියො අට දෙනා　　　　ගේ

daksạna kataka vat hāňḍa naga nagāgē

rokveṇa varala bædimal koda nurāgē

sakmaṇa gamaṇa kum̌bulela dena tumāgē

laksana kiyanu bæri liyō aṭa denāgē

6　යුතු කළ පටු නලල සරසඳ නුදුරු කො　　　ට

රතු නිලමිණි දෙනත දිසිදිළි මුකුළු ක　　　ට

මතුකල රංලියක[48] දෙසවං කණෙක කැ　　　ට

මුතුදල දෙපෙළ දිළි පිරිසිදු විදුලි වැ　　　ට

yutu kaḷa paṭu nalala sarasaňḍa nuduru koṭa

ratu nilamiṇi denata disidiḷi mukuḷu kaṭa

matukala ranliyaka desavan kaṇeka kæṭa

mutudala depeḷa diḷi pirisidu viduli væṭa

7　බොලඳ අට අඟන මුතු ගෙලෙ කර බහ　　　න

සබඳ මුවතඹර සඳ කැළුමෙකි සොබ　　　න

පැලඳ කොඳ[49] කොකුම වෙර පිණිදිය ය ගහ　　　න

ලැමඳ දිළි දෙකුඹු විදුලිය වෙති කොට　　　න

bolaňḍa aṭa aňgana mutu gele kara bahana

sabaňḍa muvatam̌bara saňḍa kæḷumeki sobana

pælaňḍa koňḍa kokuma vera piṇidiya gahana

læmeda diḷi dekum̌bu viduliya veti kotan

8　මන්මද මත් සලෙල රතඹර සේ සිළ　　　ව

පුන්සඳ යුත් අනඟි යුග දඟලා බැළ　　　ව

උන්දජ[50] කොත්යටග සැරපසලා[51] කළ　　　ව

47 ලක්ෂන BL, ලක්සන M1, ලස්සන PV

48 මුතු කල රං රියක BL, M2

49 පැලඳ කොකිඳ M1

50 උන් දඳ A1

51 කොත්යට ගශරපසලා BL

රන් රද දුනු මිටෙක තුණු ඉගලා සළ වු[52]

manmada mat salela rataṁbara sē siḷuva
punsanda yut aṅgi yuga daṅgalā bæḷuva
undaja kotyaṭaṅga særapasalā kaḷuva
ran rada dunu miṭeka tuṇu iṅgalā saḷuva

9 නිමල යුග උෟරු දණ දිළිණු සුරඟ නේ[53]

නිමල තල පතුල් රන් තඹර[54] පෙති මෙ නේ

තුමුළ වත් තරඟයට සරි වෙළ රස නේ[55]

කොමල ලඳ ලියගේ[56] රූව කියනු බැරි අ නේ

nimala yuga ūru daṇa diḷiṇu suraṅganē
nimala tala patul rantaṁbara peti menē
tumuḷa vat taraṅgayaṭa sari veḷu raṅganē
komala laṅḍa liyage ruva kiyanu bæri anē

10 අබරණ පැළඳ ජනෙලිං මුව පෙමා යු තු

පිඹ රණ රණගොස[57] කරයන වීදිඔල ඇ තු[58]

දඹරණ රිදී කොකවැල ගජ ඇතිනි ම තු

තඹරණ එමල් කැඩුමෙහි[59] රවටුනයි ඇ තු[60]

abaraṇa pæḷaṅḍa janelin muva pemā yutu
pimba raṇa raṇagosa karayana vīdiola ætu

---

[52] රන් දද දුනු මීටකතුණු A1

[53] විමල යුග උාරුදණ දිනු කසුන් මෙනේ A1

[54] නල පතුල රත් හබර BL

[55] තුමුළ වත් තරඟයට සරි වෙළ රස නේ BL, තුමුළ වත අනග යුදයට කලා මෙනේ A1

[56] ලඳගනන් A1

[57] රඟගොස A1

[58] වීදි ඇතු A1

[59] කැඩුමට A1

[60] අභරණ පැළඳ ජන ලෙන් මුව පෙමා යුතු
පිබරන ගොසර රත හංසවී අවල ඇතු
අභරණ රිදී කොකු වැල ග අනී මුතු
තබරන මල් කැඩුමට රවටුනා ඇතු PV

dam̆baraṇa ridī kokavæla gaja ætini matu
tam̆baraṇa emal kædumehi rævaṭunai ætu

11　තඹුලෙල කනක මුතුහැර ඕහණ මනහැ　　　　රා[61]
කුඹුතුල ඇතුල රණහංස විදුලි එලි ක　　　　රා[62]
ඇඹුලිය[63] වරල සිකිනිදු ගෙල කරණ නු　　　　රා
බිඹුපල[64] කියා දෙතොලට රැවටි රණ ගි　　　　රා[65]

tam̆bulela kanaka mutuhera m̆bahaṇa manaherā
kum̆butula ætula raṇahansa viduli eli karā
æm̆buliya varala sikinidu gele karaṇa nurā
bim̆bupala kiyā detolata rævaṭi raṇa girā

12　සුනික්මියා සරසඳ සපිරි උවන　　　　ට
කෙණෙක් කියා නිමවනු බැරිය රුව දු　　　　ට
මදක් වියා සර හන්ෂ[66] කළ කුඹු තුල　　　　ට
මැනික් කියා රැවටුනි උරඟු දෙනෙත　　　　ට[67]

sunikviyā sarasaňḍa sapiri uvanaṭa
keṇek kiyā nimavanu bæriya ruva duṭa
madak viyā sara hansa kaḷa kum̆bu tulaṭa
mænik kiyā rævaṭuni uraňgu denetaṭa

---

[61]　මනහරා M1, M2,

[62]　තඹුලෙල කරටලා මල්දම් ගෙන නොහැරා
කුඹුතුල ඇතුලමින් මෙන් විදුලි එලි කරා A1

[63]　ඇඹුලිය M2

[64]　බිඹුපල BL

[65]　කුඹුලේ කනක ගෙල මුතු බාන මන හැරා
අඹුලිය වරල සිකිනිදු ගෙල කරන නුරා
සුරලිය ලෙසට දිව පුර සිට එන පවරා
බිඹු තොල කියා දෙතොල රැවටී රන ගිරා PV

[66]　සැර හන්ස M1, M2

[67]　සුනික් පියා සර සඳ සපිරි උවනට
කෙණෙක් කියා නිම වනු බැරිය රුව දුට
මදක් පියා සරකර හන්ස කුඹුරට
මැනික් කියා රැවටුනි උරඟු දෙනෙතට A1

13 දෑවටුනු දිව දුහුල තුණුඉඟට සැරසි යා[68]
නොවැටුනු යුග දෙකුඹු වර[69] ලෙලෙන විදුලි යා
ගැවටුනු කංකැකුළ මදි ලිහිරඟ ඇඹරි යා[70]
රැවටුනු විධදණෝ තම සුරඹලිය කි යා[71]

dævaṭunu diva duhula tunuiṅgaṭa sæarasiyā
novæṭunu yuga dekum̆bu vara lelena viduliyā
gævaṭunu kankækuḷu madi lihiraṅga æm̆bariyā
rævaṭunu vidhadaṇō tama suram̆baliya kiyā

14 ගිහිනිය තරඟනට[72] සරිලඳ සුර ණේ ක
විහිලිය ණොම කනෙක පුංසඳ වෙනි[73] මෙතෙ ක
රැහැනියටත්[74] සනෙක රණහහන්ෂ[75] මණ දොලෙ ක
ලිහිණිය රැවටුනා වෙනි තන මඩල දැ ක

gihiniya taraṅganaṭa sarilaṅda sura ṇēka
vihiliya ṇoma kaneka punsaṅḍa veni meteka
ræhæniyaṭat saneka raṇahasha maṇa doḷeka
lihiṇiya rævaṭunā veni tana maḍala dæka

15 සල්සපු කොඳට[76] බමරණ රගණ මෙලකු නු
මල් දඹ කරටලා මුතු බහණ පලඳි නු
රැල් දිගුලට දෑකමද නුවණ කනු බො නූ[77]

---

[68] ශරසීයි BL, සැරසියා M1, M2

[69] වල A1

[70] ගැවටුනු කම් කැළ්ම දිලිහිරඟ ඇඹරි යා
රැවටුනු විදුද ණොතම සුරඹ ලිය කියා A1

[71] දෑවටුන කැම් කැලුම දිලිගිරහ ඇඹරි යා
නොවැටුනු යුග දෙකඹු වරලෙස නැපි පුලි යා
කැවටුනු කැම් කැළ්ම දිලිගිරහ ඇඹරි යා
රැවටුන විදුරසේන උන්සුරබ ලිය කියා PV

[72] තරහනට M1

[73] වන් A1

[74] රැහැනියමන් A1

[75] රණහස M1, A1, රණහන්ස M2

[76] සල් සපු කැනට A1

[77] රැල් දිගුතලට ගුරැඵන් පැමිත රැවටුනු A1

නිල් වරලෙසට රැවටුනු කින්ද[78] බකමූ   නූ[79]

salsapu koňdaṭa bamaraṇa raṅgaṇa melakunu
maldaṁba karaṭalā mutu bahaṇa paḷadinu
ræl diňgulaṭa dækamada nuvaṇa kanu bonu
nil varalesaṭa rævaṭunu kinda bakamūnu

16 භීත[80] කසුන්වත් හැඳ සැරසී සොබ   ණ
ගීත නදින් රඟ කළ කුසුමෙන්[81] හම   ණ[82]
දෑත රඟෙණන් මුද්දර මිණිසිරි සිළි   ණ[83]
නාතගෙණෙන් එළි බෑස අට දෙණ අඟ   ණ

bhīta kasunvat hæňda særasī sobaṇa
gīta nadin raṅgakaḷa kusumen hamaṇa
dæta raṇen muddara minisiri siḷiṇa
nātagaṇen elibæsa aṭa deṇa aňgaṇa

17 ලක් දුනු රැසනුරය[84] රික රංජණා   වේ
දික් ගගණුවක් ණොහැර ලදගං[85] මණා   වේ[86]
රොක් උනු සෙන් සමඟ[87] යනමං[88] සිනා   වේ
නික්මුනු ලදගනෝ යෙති වන්දනා   වේ

lak dunu ræsanuraya rika ran jaṇāvē
dik gagaṇuvak ṇohæra ladagan maṇāvē

 නිල් වරලෙසට රැවටී ආ බකමූනු A1

 සල් සපු කොඳට බම සිඳු රත හන්සලනු
මල් දම් කතක මුතු තුඩු වන නීල දිනු
රැල් වරලසට මදනා නිතර කනු බොනු
නිල් වරලසට රැවටුනෙ කිම්ද බකමූනු PV

 බීත PV, M1

 සුරමෙන් A1

 ගමණ PV

 මුද්දර සත දිලි දිලුණ PV,

 ලක් දුනු රැසනුරා PV

 උදගම් A1

 දික් ගුනුවන් තොහැර උදග වන්තවේ PV

 රොක් උනු සෙන් සෙත් සමඟ BL, රොක් උනු සෙන් සමඟ A1, M1, M2

 යතිමන් PV

rokunu sen samaṅga yanaman sināvē
nikmunu laṅḍanagaṇō yeti vandanāvē

Praising of landmarks on the route

Samanola Kanda (Adams Peak)

18 මැකුණු වරළ[89] අඳුරු සරසඳ නගර ව ර[90]
සකුණු රත දෙකුඹු විදුලිය මුකුළු ක ර
ලකුණු රත දුදුල පෙතිහල් ලැමද තු ර[91]
දකුණුදිග බලව සකිසඳ[92] සුමණ ගි ර

mækuṇu varaḷa aňduru sarasaňda nagara vara
sakuṇu rata dekum̆bu viduliya mukuḷu kara
lakuṇu rata dudula petihal læmada tura
dakuṇudiga balava sakisaňḍa sumaṇa gira

Mīgahakum̆bura

19 මුසුකර පවරණට[93] ලැම ගෝමර අතු ර
අසුකර පුව වරල බැඳිමල් බිඟු මධු ර[94]
සෙසු පුර[95] ලොව අඟණ සරිදෝ රණ ගැඹු ර[96]
පසු කරපුව ඇවිත් ලඳ මීගහ කුඹු ර[97]

---

[89] මැකුණු වල M1, M2, PV, A1
[90] නරඟ බර A1
[91] රත දුහුල පෙති ගෝමර පතර PV
[92] සඳ සකි PV
[93] පවරලා PV
[94] වැදුර PV
[95] පුර BL, M1, M2, PV, සුර A1
[96] අඟන සරිලන්තේ පවර PV
[97] මුසුකර පවරණට ලැම ගෝමර අතුර
අසුකරපන් වරල බැඳිමල් බිඟු මැදුර
සෙසුපුර ලෙද අඟන සරිනොවන ගැඹුර
පසුකරපුව ඇවිත් ලඳ මීගහකුඹුර A1

මසුකර පවරලා ලැම ගෝමර අතුර
අසුකර පවරලා බැඳිමල් බිඟු වැදුර
සෙසු සුර ලොව අඟන සරිලන්තේ පවර
පසු කරපුව ඇවිත් ලඳ මී ගහ කුඹුර PV

musukara pavaraṇaṭa lǣma gōmara atura
asukara puva varala bǣndimal biňgu madura
sesupura lova aňgaṇa saridō raṇa gǣmbura
pasu karapuva ǣvit laňḍa mīgaha kumbura

Uyanvatta

20 ලියන් රොත්ත එන යන[98] වැවු විල් ඔල ට[99]

නයන් නිත්ත රසදණ දෙනුවන් නිල ට[100]

කියන් ඇත්ත රණහන්සදි[101] මල් විල ට

උයන්වත්ත පසුකර බැස වල්පොල ට

liyan rotta ena yana vǣvu vil olaṭa

nayan nitta rasaňdaṇa denuvan nilaṭa

kiyan ǣtta ranahahsadi mal vilaṭa

uyanvatta pasukara bǣsa valpolaṭa

Valpola

21 ගෑවිය වෙර සුවඳ පිණිදිය කොඳ හම ණ

පෑවිය සඳ උවණ යුගදඟ මිණි[102] නදි ණ

බෝවිය ලෑම රතැඟ පෙනි නිලඹර දෙත ණ[103]

යා විය ලඳගනෝ[104] වල්පොල පසු කර ණ

gǣviya vera suvaňda piṇidiya koňda hamaṇa

pǣviya saňda uvaṇa yugadaňga miṇi nadiṇa

bōviya lǣma rataňga peni nilambara detaṇa

yāviya laňḍaganō valpola pasu karaṇa

---

[98] රොත්ත එන BL රොත්ත එන යන M1, M2, රොත්ත යන මග PV

[99] වලට A1

[100] ගොයම් නිත්ත රස දෙනුවන් නීලවට PV

[101] රණ හසදි M1, A1 රණ හන්ෂදි BL

[102] පිනි PV

[103] බෝවිය ලෑම රතඟ නිලඹර දෙත වරුත PV බාවිය ලෑමර තැගපෙති නිලඹර දෙතත A1

[104] ලඳ ලියෝ A1, PV

Kaḍavata Kælē

22	තුඩ රත්තඹර පෙති පියයුරු පානු ණ	මා[105]
	වැඩ අන[106] දිඟුවරල බැඳිමල් රේණු යො	මා
	දිඩ කන මොණ සලෙල[107] පිණි දිය ගානු තෙ	මා
	කඩවත කැලේ පසුකර යනවාළු ළ	මා

tuḍa ratatam̆bara peti piyayuru pānu ṇamā

væḍa ana diǹguvarala bæ̆ndimal rēnu yomā

diḍa kana moṇa salela piṇidiya gānu temā

kaḍavata kælē pasukara yanavāḷu ḷamā

Kollægala

23	නිල්ලා දිඟු වරල බැඳිමල් කොඳ සොදු	ර
	ලොල්ලා වණ සලෙල[108] රතඹර සේ ගොදු	ර[109]
	දුල්ලා දල කමල සඳවෙනි බිඳි අඳු	ර[110]
	කොල්ලැගලට[111] බැස වඳු පස්ඇස මදු	ර[112]

nillā diǹgu varala bæ̆ndimal koǹda sodura

lollā vaṇa salela ratam̆bara sē godura

dullā dala kamala saǹḍaveni bin̆di an̆dura

kollægalaṭa bæsa van̆du pasæsa madura

24	සල්සපු කීන අඹ දොඹ මිඅඹ පළො	ලී
	දෙල් මොර කැන්ද සුවිසල් සොඳ නා මිදෙ	ලී
	තල කිතුලින්ද පොල් පුවකිඟු එසලි ම	ලී
	මල්කැළ බරින් සැදිතුරු කැල බලනු ලො	ලී

---

[105] කුඹ රතබර පෙති පියයුරු බානු තමා PV කුඩ රන් තඹර පෙති පියයුරු බානු තමා A1

[106] කැඩ අත PV මැඩ අත A1

[107] වැඩ කත මෙන සලෙලු PV දිඩ කත මෝ සලෙල A1

[108] ලොල්ලා වත සලෙල A1 ලොල්ලා වන සලෙලු රතබර ලා ගොදුර PV

[109] සොදුර A1

[110] උල්ලා සදක මල සදවැනි බිඟු මැදුර PV දුල්ලා දල කමල සදවැනි බිඟු අඳුර A1

[111] වැල්ලා ගලට PV

[112] බැස වැදු පසු ඇත මැදුර PV

salsapu kīna am̌ba dom̌ba mīam̌ba paḷolī
del mora kænda suvisal sonda na midelī
tala kitulinda pol puvakingu esali malī
malkæla barin sædituru kæla balanu lolī

25　මුනිඳු අපා බුදුවී වැඩ සිටි අයු　රෑ
　　පසිඳු ඉතා කරනෙවි බෝමුල සොඳු　රෑ
　　සුසැඳු අපා මුනිවරු දැකගොස් සොඳු　රෑ
　　නමඳු ළඳා සිහිකර නවගුණ මතු　රෑ

munidu apā buduvī væḍa siṭi ayuru
pasin̆du itā karanevu bomula son̆duru
susædu apā munivaru dækagos son̆duru
namadu ḷan̆dā sihikara navaguṇa maturu

Batupiṭigama

26　වටු ශටි[113] පටු නලල දිසි මුතු ලා බෙල්　ළ
　　තුටු මිටි රණ් රඹණ කුඩු තුරු[114] ගැවිල්　ළ
　　දුටු සිටි[115] සඳ සලෙල කරවට ලා තැල්　ළ
　　බටුපිටිගමින් යන ලඳ[116] අඟනෝ ගොල්　ළ

vaṭu śaṭi paṭu nalala disi mutu lā bella
tuṭu miṭi raṇ ram̌baṇa kudu turu gævilla
duṭu siṭi san̆da salela karavaṭa lā tælla
baṭupiṭigamin yana lan̆da an̆ganō golla

Randenivæla

27　තැල්ල පුරා කරලාලා[117] පොට දෙපො　ට

---

[113]　වටු සැටි A1 පට සැම් PV

[114]　රණ් තඹර කඹු තුරැ A1, තුටු විට රත්තඹර කුඹුරන PV

[115]　දුටු විට PV

[116]　බටු පිටි ගමින් යන ලඳ A1 බටු පිටි ගම වෙලේ යන PV

[117]　තැල්ල පුරා කරලා කරලා BL, තැල්ල පුරාලා කරලා A1, තැල්ල පුරාලා කරවට
　 PV

බෙල්ල තුරා රනහන්ෂ කුඹු[118] පෙති පෙල · · · ට

දුල්ල සළු සඟල හැඳ නිලඹර රණ · · · ට[119]

ගොල්ල ලියෝ ගොස් බෑස[120] රංදෙනිවෙල · · · ට

tælla purā karalālā poṭa depoṭa

bella nurā ranahansha kumbu peti pelaṭa

dulla saḷu saṅgal hæṅḍa nilambara raṇaṭa

golla liyō gos bæsa randenivælaṭa

28 ලංවුනි ගෙවතු තල් තල පොහො සංඹල · · · ම

ගංමිණි සිරි සිහිල් ගෝගවයිං තල · · · ම

ටැන් තනිවන් කොකිනි උළු සේවෙලිං කැළ · · · ම

රංදෙනිවෙලේ ගලපිට සෑදු[121] අම්ඹල · · · ම[122]

lanvuni gevatu tal tala poho sanmbalama

ganmiṇi siri sihil gōgavayin talama

ṭæn tanivan kokini uḷu sēvelin kæḷuma

randenivælē galapiṭa sædu ambalama

Yakdessā Kanda

29 රිලාවන් වදුරු උකු බස්සා වූ · · · න්ද

වලාකැන් බුරණ රූපු රැස්සා වෙ · · · න්ද

මුලාකැන් කරණ මුව කැස්සාගු · · · න්ද

බලාපන් මිතුර යද්දෙස්සාක · · · න්ද[123]

---

[118] රනහස කුඹු A1 බෙල්ල තුරා රනහස කුඹු PV

[119] රඟට A1 දුල්ල සළු සගල ඇද නිලඹර රතට PV

[120] ගොල්ල ලියෝ ගොස්වෙනි A1 ගොල්ල ලියෝ ගොස් වන් PV

[121] ශදු BL සෑදු M1, M2

[122] ලං වුනි ගෙවතු තල් පොල් කොස් අම්බලම
ගොන් මිනි සිරි සලින ගොන් ගවයින් තලම
මන්තනි වත් කොතින් උලු ගෙවලින් කැලම
රන් දෙනි වෙලේ ගලපිට සෑදි අම්බලම PV

[123] රිලාවන් වදුරු උකු බස්සා උන්ද
බලා කැන් බුරණ රූදු බළ දියන්ද
මෙලා කෑ කරණ මුව කැස්සා උන්ද

rilāvan vaṅduru uku bassā vunda
valākæn buraṇa rupu ræssā venda
mulakæn karaṇa muva kæssā gunda
balāpan mitura yaddessākanda

30

කතුර සිත් පිනවන තුරු පෙලින් සැ   දි
ඉටුවන ලෙසින් ගියවුන් මන කොඳ පුබු   දි
තුටුවන තුරින් බබලන හෙලගිර සබ   දි
දුටුදන සිත් අදනට හැකි මා සබ   දි

duṭudana sit pinavana turu pelin sædi
iṭuvana lesin giyavun mana koňda pubudi
tuṭuvana turin babalana helagira sabaňdi
duṭu dana sit adanaṭa hæiki mā sabaňdi

Doḷu Kanda

31

කතුර දිගු තුඩණර රණ[124] රත කළ ඇ   න්දි[125]
යතුර කර හඬිං දිවි කුළ පොළ හ   න්දි[126]
අතර තුර රඟන කොකවැල දිළි කු   න්ද
මිතුර බල ඉහරු දිග දිලි දොළ ක   න්දි[127]

බලා පන් මිතුරෙ යද්දෙස්සා කන්ද A1
රිලාවන් වදුරු උකුබස් සාවුන්ද
බලා කැන් බුරන රූපු රැස්සා මෙන්ද
මුලා කැකරනා මුව වස්සා මෙන්ද
බලා පන් මිතුර යක් දෙස්සා කන්ද PV
[124] තුඩණර රණ BL තුඩැර රණ රත M1, M2
[125] කතුර දිගු තුන්ඩර ණර රත්නක ළු ඇන්ද A1
[126] යතුර කරහනින් දිවි කුළ පොළ හන්ද A1
[127] කතර දිගු තුන්ඩ ගන රන් පොලු ඇන්ද
යතුර කර නින්ද දිලු කුලු පොලු ඇන්ද
අතර තුරගනෝ කොකක වැල දිලි කුන්ද
මිතුර බල ඉදුර දිග ඇත දොලු කන්ද PV

කතුර දිගු තුන්ඩ රන රන් තක ලු ඇන්ද
යතුර කර හනින්ද දිවිකුලු පොලු හන්ද
අතර තුර රඟන කොක වැල දිලි කුන්ද
සොදුර බල ඉදුරු දිග දිලි දොලු කන්ද A1

katura diṅgu tuḍaṇara raṇa rata kaḷu ænda
yatura kara haṅdin divi kuḷu poḷu handa
atara tura raṅgana kokavæla diḷi kunda
mitura bala iharudiga dili doḷu kanda

32 පෙර විසු දැහැමි රජදරුවෝ සිත් තුටි   න

පර වැඩ නොව තම වැඩ මෙන් කර තිබෙ   න

දුර නොව අසල පින් සලකන දන සිටි   න

කර පිණිපා යවු නවගුණ සිහි කර   න

peravisu dæhæmi rajadaruvō sit tuṭina
para væḍa nova tama væḍa men kara tibena
dura nova asala pin salakana dana siṭina
kara piṇipā yavu navaguṇa sihi karana

Dunupataṅga

33 ගත්තන් සළු වැලඳ බඳමුතු ගෙත්ත   ග

යන්නන් සිලි කෙළිණ කුඹුතුරු කොත්නෑ   ග

වන්නන් මුතු දෙපෙල දලරණ රත්ත   ග

යන්නන් ලියෝ පසුකර දුනුපත්ත   ග[128]

gattan saḷu vælaṅda baṅdamutu gettaṅga
yannan sili keḷiṇa kumbuturu kotaṅga
vannan mutu depala dalaraṇa rattaṅga
yannan liyō pasu kara dunupataṅga

---

[128] ගන්න සළු වැලඳ ලඳ මුතු නෙත් අන්ග
යන්නන් සිරිසලින කුඹුතුරු නෙත් අන්ග
ගොනතන් මුතු දෙපොට ලඳ රන රත් අන්ග
යන්නන් ලියෝ පසු කර දුනු පත් අන්ග   PV

ගන්නන් සළු වැලඳ බඳ මුතු ගෙත් තන් ග
යන්නන් සිලිකෙලින කුඹුතුරු කොත් තැන් ග
වන්නන් මුතු දෙපෙල ලඳ රත රත් තැන් ග
යන්නන් ලියා පසු කර දුනු පත් අන් ග   A1

Vallāgala

34 රතැස් නුවණ් රතඹර නිල්ලා නෙත ට[129]

සිලැස් කතුන් වනහැඳ[130] එල්ලා වම ට

අදැස් කොමින් පිනිදිය ගල්ලා ලැම ට

පසැස්මැදුර[131] දැක වඳු වල්ලාගල ට[132]

rætæs nuvaṇ ratambara nillā netaṭa

silæs katun vanahæṅda ellā vamaṭa

adæs komin pinidiya gallā læmaṭa

pasæsmædura dæka vaṅdu vallāgalaṭa

35 නිල්ලාවත සොම්පුල්ලා ලඳ ලැමතුල තැ ල්ල[133]

තෙල්ලා ඉස පැටලිල්ලා වරලෙස ගැවසි ල්ල

නිල්ලා වත[134] රැලි අල්ලා රණහන්ෂ නැවි ල්ල[135]

වැල්ලාගල දැකපල්ලා මිතුරේ[136] පුරණ ල්ල

nillāvata somipullā laṅda læmatula tælla

tellā isa pæṭalillā varalesa gævasilla

nillā vata ræli allā raṇahanṣa nǣvilla

vællāgala dækapallā miturē puraṇalla

36 මුනිඳු ඉතා සුළු කුසිනාරා නුව ර

පසිඳු ඉතා කරනෙව් සල්තුරු අත ර

දිනුදු ලෙසා පිරිනිවී මුනි රූ අය ර

නමඳු මෙතා සිහිකර අනිත පදස ර

muniṅdu itā suḷu kusināra nuvara

<hr>

[129] රතැස් නුවන් රතඹර නිල්ලා කෙතට A1

[130] කසුන් වත හැඳ A1

[131] මදුර BL මැදුර M1, M2

[132] රහැන් නුවන් රතඹර නිල්ලා නෙතට
විලැස් කසුන් වත් ඇඳ එල්ලා වමට
ඇදැස් කමින් පිනිදිය ගල්ලා ලැමට
පසැස් මැදුර දැක වැඳු වැල්ලාගලට PV

[133] ලොල්ලා වත සොම්පුල්ලා ලඳ ලැම තැල්ල A1, තුල බෙල්ල M1

[134] අල්ලා වත M1

[135] රණ හස නැලවිල්ල A1 රණ හස නෑවිල්ල M1 රණ හංස නෑවිල්ල M2

[136] අගණෙනි A1

pasiňdu itā karanevu salturu atara
diniňdu lesā pirinivi muni rū ayura
namaňdu metā sihikara anita padasara

37

මතුවැඩ තකා වැඳ මැදුරින් නික්ම සි ට
යුතු මතු ගමන් ඇති පෙරමග බලා සි ට
නතු තෙවරක් කොට සකිසඳ බැස මග ට
කතුනි සැවොම යවු වෙහෙරින් නික්ම තු ට

matuvæḍa takā vaňda mædurin nikma siṭa

yutumatu gaman æti peramaga balā siṭa

natu tevarak koṭa sakisaňda bæsa magaṭa

katuni sævoma yavu veherin nikma tuṭa

Mudannāpola

38

නොදන්නා බොළඳ ලිය කෙළි කවට ලි ය[137]
අදින්නා සළුව තුනු ඉඟවටට ලි ය
එදන්නා කොමට තුඹු කෙළි විදුලි සි ය
මුදන්නාපොලත් පසුකර මෙළඳ ගි ය

nodannā boḷaňda liya keḷi kavaṭa liya

adinnā saḷuva tunu iňgavaṭaṭa liya

edannā komaṭa tuṁbu keḷi viduli siya

mudannāpolat pasukara melaňda giya

39

රැල්ලලා සළුව සිහිනිඟට තිල්ල ලා
තෙල්ලලා බැඳපු නිල්වරල එල්ල ලා
බෙල්ලලා එරණ් දඹ කරට තැල්ල ලා[138]
සොල්ලලා කතුන් ඇති දෙකුඹු සොල්ල ලා

rællalā saḷuva sihiniňgaṭa tillalā

tellalā bæňḍapu nilvarala ellalā

bellalā eraṇ daṁba karaṭa tællalā

---

[137] කෙළි කවට අය A1
[138] එරන් දම කර තැලෙල්ලා A1

sollalā katun eti dekum̌bu sollalā

40 මලාලිත සුවිසාලා ලඳ කුඹුජාලා රතන් ග[139]
දීලා ලඳ කරලාලා මුතු හැරලාලා අන ග[140]
ගාලා පිණිදිය පැලා කුඹු සරසාලා එක ග[141]
වේලාගල දළදාළා එති සැරසීලා[142] මේම ග

malālita suvisālā lan̆da kum̌bujālā ratan̆ga
dīlā lan̆da karalālā mutu hæralālā anan̆ga
gālā pinidiya pælā kum̌bu sarasālā ekan̆ga
vēlāgala daḷadāḷa eti særasīlā meman̆ga

41 ගංඟා ජලරැල නැඟා මුහුලස ශ්‍රිඟා බොළ ඳ
තුඟා කොඳරණ රඟා මුතුදජ[143] නැඟා එල ඳ
පඟා බමනොම සඟා පිය කොමල ඟා පැල ඳ
රඟාලිය කර නැඟා කුඹුතුරු තුඟා මෙල ඳ

gan̆gā jalaræla næn̆ga muhulasa shrin̆gā boḷan̆da
tun̆gā kon̆daraṇa ran̆gā mutudaja næn̆gā elan̆ga
pan̆gā bamanoma san̆gā piya komala n̆gā pælan̆da
ran̆gāliya kara næn̆gā kum̌buturu tun̆gā melan̆da

42 සඟා[145] රණලිය කඟා සළැඳ නඟා දැරූ ව
අඟා නොම රතිරඟා නෙතදුන ලඟා තඹු ව
ගැඟා ලැම එක දඟාකොද පෙති පෙඟා තිබු ව[146]

---

139 කුඹු සාලා රත්තෑඟ A1 රතඟ M1, M2

140 මුතුහැරලාලා අතන්ඟ BL මුතුහැරලාලා අනඟ M1, M2

141 සරසාලා එකන්ඟ BL සරසාලා එකඟ M1, M2, සරසා ලා එ ඇඟ A1

142 මේලාගල දඟලාලා එති සරසාලා A1, ශරසීලා BL සැරසීලා M1, M2

143 දඞ BL දඣ M1, M2

144 ගන් ජල හා රැල නැන්ඟා මුහුලසයින් ඟා බොළඳ
තුන්ඟා කොඳ රණ ඟා මුතු දඳ නැන්ඟි මෙන් රත් ලඳ
පන්ඟා ධම් නොවසන් ඟා ලියනොවලන් ඟා පැලඳ
රන්හා ලිය කර තැන් ඟා කුඹුතුරු තැන්ඟා මෙලඳ A1

145 සන්ඹා M2

146 පෙති පෙං තිබුව M1 පෙති ඔා තිබුව M2

රඔාලිය නුඔෙ කුඔා පියයුරු බඔා ඇඹු ^{147} ව

samba ranaliya kamba saḷuæňḍa namba dæruva
amba noma ratiramba netaduna lamba tambuva
gæmba læma eka dambākoda peti pemba tibuva
rambāliya numbe kumba piyayuru bamba ambuva

Māňguru Oya

43

මුගුරු සිපත් ගෙණ පෙරටුව සහ සොඔ   න
අගුරු තෙලින් ඇදිපෙති සුගුබලා තැ   න
අගුරු වලළුසේ කුඩමසු වෑගා   න
මාගුරුඔය පසුව යන ලද අසමා   න ^{148}

muňguru sipat gena peraṭuva saha sobana
aňguru telin ædipeti sugubalā tæna
aňguru valaḷusē kuḍamasu vǣgāna
māňguruoya pasuva yana laňda asamāna

Aḷupotagan Vǣla

44

සළුගත දිගුවරල බැදිමල් බිගු පත   ර
දිළුරත මදකුමුදු බඳපිය කුඹුල ක   ර
කළුරන් තුඩු කැකුළු ^{149} ගෝ්මර ^{150} පෙති පත   ර

---

^{147} සන්ඔා රණ ලිය කම්ඔා සළුහැද නන්ඔා දැරුව
අන්ඔා නොම රති රන්ඔා නෙත අතලන් ඔා තැබ්ඔුව
ගැන්ඔා ලෑම එකදන් කොද පෙති පෙම්ඔා තිබ්ඔුව
රන්ඔා ලිය නුඔෙ කුන්ඔා පියයුරු බම්ඔා ඇම්ඔුව A1

^{148} මුගුරු සිපාගෙණ පෙරටිව සසොබාණ
අගුරු තෙලින් ඇදිපෙති සුගුබල නෑණ
අගුරු වලළ කුඩ මසු මෙහි වෑගාණ
මගුරු ඔය පසුව යන ලද අසමාණ A1

මගුරු සිපන් ඉගෙන පෙරටුව සසහාන
අගුරු තෙලිය ඇදි යුග පෙති බලපාන
ගිගුරු වලලු කුඩ මසු වැලි ගග පාන
මගුරු ඔය පසුව යන ලද අසමාන PV

^{149} කළු රත කෑඹු කැකුල A1
^{150} ගෝ්බර BL ගෝ්මර M1, M2, A1, PV

අළුපොතගන්වෙලෙන් යන ලද බල[151] මිතු ර[152]

saḷugata diṅguvarala baṅdimal biṅgu patara
diḷurata madakumudu baṅḍapiya kuṁbula kara
kaḷuran tudu kækuḷu gōmara peti patara
aḷupotaganvelen yana laṅda bala mitura

45 සොඳුරු රුවැති කුමරුන් ඇකයෙහිම ත බා
මියුරු හඬින් කියමින් කවි ගී නොත බා
මහරු බැතින් පතිදන් පුරන සිත ත බා
සොඳුරු රුවැති අඟනුන් යන ගමන් සු බා

soṅduru ruvæti kumarun ækayehima tabā
miyuru haṅdin kiyamin kavi gī notabā
maharu bætin patidan purana sita tabā
soṅduru ruvæti aṅganun yana gaman subā

46 නිල් මේකුලෙව් වරලස උනමින් දිග ට
ඇල් මේ සිතින් සලෙලුන් දෙස විටින් වි ට
බැලුන් ලමින් සිටි ඒ වරගණන් හ ට
බැලුම් එවොත් බඹසරවත් කැදෙයි දු ට

nil mekulevu varalasa unamin digata
ælme sitin salelun desa vitin vita
bælum lamin siti ē varaṅgaṇan hata
bælum evot bambasaravat kædeyi duta

47 සොඳුරු රුවින් දිසි පුන්සඳ වන් වතැ තී

---

[151] යන මෙලද බල මිතුර BL යන ලද බල මිතුර A1, M2, යන කත බල මිතුර M1,

[152] සඵගත දිගු වරල බැදිමල් බිඟු පතර
දිලුරත මද කුමල බදවට මුකුලු කර
කුලු රත කුබු කැකුලු ගෝමර පෙති පතර
අලු පොතු ගම වෙලෙන් යන ලද බල මිතුර PV

සඵගත දිගු වරල බැදිමල් බිඟු පතර
දිඵරත මද කුමුද බදුපිය කුඹුලකකර
කළ රත කුඹු කැකුල ගෝමර පෙති පතර
අළ පොතු ගම් වෙලෙන් යන ලද බල මිතුර A1

තියුණු නැණින් පවසන සොඳ කතා ඇ   ති

මියුරු හඬින් ගී තුති කවි කියන නි   ති

ළදරු උමාවන් රූ ඇති අඟණ යෙ   ති

soňduru ruvin disi punsaňda van vatæti

tiyunu naṇin pavasana soňda katā æti

miyuru haňdin gi tuti kavi kiyana niti

ḷadaru umāvan rū æti aňgaṇa yeti

Vilgandemata Væva

48 පුල් රන්වන් ලැමැද දිළි මුතුහර ණග   ණ[153]

තැල්මෙන් සැදී දෙතන රනහස මුර රග   ණ[154]

මල්කැන් වර බොලඳ කත යුගදඟ ඉග   ණ

විල්ගන්දෙමට වැව පසුකර යන අග   ණ[155]

pul ratvan læmæda diḷi mutuhara ṇagaṇa

tælmen shadi detana ranahasa mura raňgaṇa

malkæn vara bolaňḍa kata yugadaňga iňgaṇa

vilgandemaṭa væva pasukara yana aňgaṇa

Balaḷuvāgāra

49 එළළුවා ඇඟට පෙති තඹර සැළසු   නෝ[156]

නිල්ළුවා රතට සළ වැලඳ දිළි සු   නෝ

වලළලා යුගත සිරි සිලිනි[157] නඳ දු   නෝ

---

153 න (all lines ending with)

154 තැල්මෙන් ශදී දෙතන රනහන්ෂ මුර රගණ BL

155 දුල්ල රන් ලැමැද දිලිමුතු රන් බරන
 තැල්මෙන් සැදී දෙතන රනහස මුතු ගාන
 මල් කැම් වර බොලඳ කතයුග දග ඉගෙන
 විල්ගම් දෙබට වැව පසුකර යන අඟන PV

 පුල් රන්වන් ලැමැද දිලිමුතු හර බහන
 කැල්මෙන් සදිසි තනරනහස මුරුතගන
 මල් කැන් බොලඳ කත යුග දග මෙන් ඉගන
 විල්ගම් දෙමට වැව පසුකර යන අඟන A1

156 ශළසුනෝ BL (also ending all the lines with නො) සැළසුනෝ M1, M2

157 සිලි සිලිනි M1

බලළුවාගාරයෙන් යේ එළඳ ග   නො[158]

eḷaḷuvā æṅgaṭa peti taṁbara sæḷasuṇō
nilaḷuvā rataṭa saḷu vælaṅḍa diḷi suṇō
valaḷulā yugata siri silini naṅda duṇō
balaḷuvāgārayen yē elaṅḍa gaṇō

Tissō Væla

50   ඉස්සෝ ලැමද පෙති ගෝමර[159] ලඳුන්   නේ
       විස්සෝපයෙන් ලඳගනෝ පිං කරන්   නේ
       උස්සෝ පියාසර සාසළ ලඳුන්   නේ[160]
       තිස්සෝවෙලට[161] එපිටිං ගම යොනුන්   නේ

issō læmada peti gōmara laṅdunnē
vissōpayen laṅḍagaṇō pin karannē
ussō piyāsara sāsaḷu laṅdunnē
tissōvelaṭa epiṭin gama yonunnē

Yongama

51   සකිසඳ තොපි ගොස් සිට ඒ ගමට වැ   ද
       හැකි ලෙසකින් තම කිසකර යව් සබ   ද
       මකියන ලෙසින් ඒ ගම වැද නොසිට තො   ද
       සකිලිය අනේ යව යොන්ගම පසුව ඉ   ද

sakisaṅda topi gos siṭa ē gamaṭa væda

---

[158] එල්ලු වා ඇඟට පෙති ගෝම්‍ර ඉසුනේ
නිලලුවා රතට නිල්සලුව දිළි සුනේ
වළලු ලා අතට සිරි සිලුත නඳලුනේ
බලලුවා අනාරෙන් යත්ලු ලඳ ගනේ PV

එල එ වා ඇඟට පෙතිතඹර සැලසුනෝ
නිල එ වා රතට සළ්වැලඳ දිළි සුනෝ
වළ එ ලා යුගත සිරි සිලි නඳ තැඩුනෝ
බල එ වා අඟාරෙන් යෙති එළඳ ගනෝ A1

[159] ගෝඹර BL

[160] පියාසර කරනා ලෙසින් නේ A1

[161] කිස්සෝ ගමට PV

hæki lesakin tama kisakara yavu sambaňda
makiyana lesin ē gama væda nosiṭa toda
sakilya ane yava yongama pasuva iňda

Sērugolla

52
සීරුබෙල්ල වට මුතුරන්[162] කොදෙකු[163] න මා
ගෝරුවැල්ල පිණිදිය රන් බඳට තෙ මා
මාරුලොල්ල පිරිසිදු කත සේම ත මා[164]
සේරුගොල්ල පසුකර යනවාද ල මා[165]

sīrubella vaṭa yuturan kodeku namā
gōruvælla pinidiya ran baňḍaṭa temā
marulolla pirisidu kata sēma tamā
sērugolla pasukara yanavāda lamā

53
සුරඟනවන් රූ ඇති අඟනන් විසි න
සුමදුර ලෙසින් දෙන ඔවදන් සිතට ගෙ න
දල සිළුවන් නෙත් සඟලින් බැලුම් ල න
සමර ලෙසින් සිටි තරුණන් හැරෙව් යි න

suraňganavan rū æti aňganan visina
sumadura lesin dena ovadan sitaṭa gena
dala siḷuvan net saňgalin bælum lana
samara lesin siṭi taruṇan hærevu yina

Nuvara Kanda

54
පවරබැන්ද ගිරි සිලි තුරු ණගර ව ර

කවරකින්ද ගිරි කුළු කඳු අනඟ ව   ර[166]
මෙවර කින්ද ගිරි ලෙන මුනි දකින ව   ර[167]
නුවරකන්ද බලසකි සඳ[168] නැගෙනහි   ර[169]

pavarabænda giri sili turu ṇagara vara

kavarakinda giri kuḷu kaňdu anaṅga vara

mevara kinda giri lena muni dakina vara

nuvarakanda balasaki saňḍa negenahira

55 මුරුකැල වසන තුරුපෙල සදිසි වන් එයි   න

තුරුදෙස බලා මනතුටු කරමින් සොඳි   න

සුරුව තමන් කටයුතු අනලස වෙමි   න

මරුගේ අඟනුන්ට සමවන් තොපි යමි   න

murukæla vasana turupela sadisi van eyina

turudesa balā manatuṭu karamin soňdina

suruva taman kaṭayutu analasa vemina

maruge aňganunṭa samavan topi yamina

Dæduru Oya

56 වීදුරු වැලිත් නිලඹර ජල සලා දෙ   න

ගොදුරු මසුං රැලි දියපිට පිනා එ   න

තොදුරු අනත කෙළ කෙළ යෙති සිනාසෙ   න

දැදුරුඹයෙන් නානා ලද නා නය   න[170]

---

[166] කුළු තද අඟන වර A1

[167] ගිරි කුලෙ මුනිදක නවර A1

[168] බල සඳ A1

[169] පවර බැන්ද නිල් සිරි තුරුනගර වර
කවර කින්ද ගිරි කුලු කුඩු අගනුව ර
මෙවර කිම්ද ගිරි ලෙන මුනිදා දැකවර
නුවර කන්ද බල සකි නැගෙනහිර PV

[170] වීදුරු වැලිත් නිලඹර පෙල සලා එන
ගොදුරු මසුන් වැලි පරදා ගීනයන
නපුරු අඟන කෙළ කෙළ යන සිනාසෙන
දැදුරු ඔයෙන් නානා ලදගනෝ යන PV

vīduru vælit nilam̌bara jala salā dena
goduru masun ræli diyapiṭa pinā ena
noduru anata keḷa keḷa yeti sināsena
dæduruoyen nānā laňḍa nā nayana

57

මෙසේ සකිනි ඒ මග පසුකර යමි   න
කෙසේ වුවත් එහි නොරැඳි යවු කල   න
තොසේ සිතින් මා ඔවදන් සිත් තුලි   න
කෙසේ වුවත් නොකරව බැහැර පියඟ   න

mese sakini ē maga pasukara yamina
kese vuvat ehi noraňdi yavu kalana
tose sitin mā ovadan sit tulina
kese vuvat nokarava bæhæra piyaňgana

58

සිරි ලකඟන මතුයෙහි කෙලිනා සෙයි   න
කිරිවන් පඬෙර සුබකුල උපන් සොඳඟ   න
සිරිනෙක වොරැඳි දුටුවන් සිත් සතුටු ව   න
සිරිකත වන් අඟනුනි යවු නැඟ එයි   න

siri lakaňgana matuyehi kelinā seyina
kirivan paňdera subakula upan soňdaňgana
sirineka voraňdi duṭuvan sit satuṭu vana
sirikata van aňganuni yavu næga eyina

Nindagama

59

නිලවැල්ලේ[171] සල්ව තුෂු ඉග ඇන්ද ත   මා[172]
විල මැද රත්තඹර පෙති මුවගින්ද පෙ   මා
රල මැද සිදු හමණ සිසිරණ වින්ද ත   මා[173]

විදුරැ වලින් නිලඹර ජල සලා හෙත
තොදුරැ ඔවුන් තිතිනා තාතතායෙන
නුදුරැ අගන කෙල කෙල යෙති සිතාසෙන
දැදුරැ ඔයෙන් බස්නා ජල නතා යෙන A1
[171] නළ වැද A1
[172] නල වැද ලෙල සලුව තුනු ඉග ඇන්ද ලමා PV
[173] සිසි මුව වින්ද ලමා A1 සිසිලන වින්ද ලමා PV

වෙලමැද අම්බලම බලසකි නින්ද ග   මා

nilavællē saḷuva tuṇu iṅga ænda namā
vila mæda rattam̌bara peti muvaginda pemā
ræla mæda sidu hamaṇa sisiraṇa vinda tamā
velamæda amm̌balama balasaki ninda gamā

60   මනකල් තෙරුවනෙහි බැති සිතති දනව   ර
       සැමකල් පැමිණ ගිමහැරුමට කල පව   ර
       මනදුල් වන එමැදුර සිට ගිමන් හැ   ර
       තොපි ලොල් නොවී එතනින් යව තව බැහැ   ර

manakal teruvanehi bæti sitati danavara
sæmakal pæmiṇa gimahærumaṭa kala pavara
manadul vana emædura siṭa giman hæra
topi lol novī etænin yava tava bæhæra

Divulvæva

61   මෙවුල් දඹ වැලදී ලඳ තුනු ඉඟ කොහො   මා[174]
       අවුල් බිඳපු[175] රණ් රද දුනු මිට මහි   මා
       දවුල් බෙර මොරහු[176] පෙරටුව යන කළ   මා
       දිවුල්වැට මීං බටු අඟනෝ තල   මා[177]

mevul dam̌ba væladī laňda tunu iṅga kohomā
avul biňḍapu raṇ rada dunu miṭa mahimā
davul bera morahu peraṭuva yana kaḷamā
divulvævaṭa min baṭu aňgaṇō talamā

62   තැන තැන හිඳන ගිතුති කියමින් රඟ   ණ

---

[174] ම instead of මා for all four lines A1
[175] අවුල් කරපු A1
[176] මොවුන් A1
[177] මෙවුල් ලඳ වැලදී ලඳ තුනු ඩග කොහොමා
අවුල් බිඳ පු රන් රද දුණු ඉග කොහොමා
කොවුල් බෙර මොරහු පෙරටුව යත කලමා
දිවුල් වැවට විත් බටු අඟනෝ කල මා PV

ළඳගන රඟ බලමින් සිත් තුටු වෙමි   ණ

දැනමන තුටින සවනත කරනෙවු කල   ණ

රඟදෙන රඟ බලමින් යව තව එයි   ණ

tæna tæna hiṅdana gituti kiyamin raṅgaṇa

ḷaṅdagana raṅga balamin sit tuṭu vemiṇa

dænamana tuṭina savanata karanevu kalaṇa

raṅgadena raṅga balamin yava tava eyiṇa

63 දුටු දැන සිත් පොබකළ සොඳ කමල් ව   න්

තුටුවෙයි දුටු දනන් තුනුරුසිරු රන්ව   න්

තුටු පහටුව සමර යුදයට එවුව මෙ   න්

දුටුවන් සිත් තුටුවෙයි අඟනුන් රන්ව   න්

duṭu dæna sit pobakaḷa soṅda kamal van

tuṭuvei duṭu daṅan tunurusiru ranvan

tuṭu pahaṭuva samara yudayaṭa evuva men

duṭuvan sit tuṭuvæi aṅganun ranvan

64 නීති පලගත් මෙපියස පොල්තුරු රස   ය

නල වැදගත් කල ලෙලදෙන සොඳ ලෙස   ය

සොඳ දරුවන් ගත් අඟනුන් සිටි ලෙස   ය

තට මනරන් ගත් මෙන් දක්වයි පිරි   ය

niti palagat mepiyasa polturu rasaya

nala vædagat kala leladena soṅda lesaya

soṅda daryvan gat aṅganun siṭi lesaya

taṭa manaran gat men dakvai piriya

Kim̆bulvāna Oya

65 ඇඹුල් රුක් වීර පළ මොරද දුටු ද   තො

බුබුල් ජල පතර පත් ගැඹුර ණොතැමු   තො

තුඹුල් දඹ සපිරි නිල් සළ්ව ගැ‍‍වෙසු   තෝ[178]

---

[178] තුඹුල් බඳ සපිරි නිල් සළ්ව ඇඹරුතො A1

කිඹුල්වාණ ඔය පසු කරපු ලඳ ග   තො[179]

æm̆bul ruk vīra paḷu morada duṭu daṇō
bubul jala patara pat gæm̆bura ṇotæmuṇō
tum̆bul dam̆ba sapiri nil saḷuva gævasuṇō
kim̆bulvāṇa oya pasukarapu laňda gaṇō

Handapāngama

66 නෙකතුන් වෙර සළ්වලා ලඳ රැන්ද   ම

මෙකතුන් තුසර මුව දිසි දිළි කාන්ද   ම

තකදොන් කුඹු ලෙලෙණ විතරග මෙන්දහ   ම

දැකපන් මිතුර මේ වෙල හඳපාන්ග   ම[180]

nekatun vera saḷuvalā laňda rændama
mekatun tusara muva disi diḷi kāndama
takadon kum̆bu leleṇa viharaga mendahama
dækapan mitura mē vela handapānňgama

Kirilāgedara

67 පැන්නා දියෙන් පීනා තිසරන නිත   ර

දෙන්නා ලැය රන හන්සවි දුර පත   ර

ඇන්න ගියේ පෙන්නා සලසල ගොදු   ර

මෙන්න ලියේ දැකපන් කිරිලා ගෙද   ර

pænna diyen pinā tisarana nitara

---

179 ඇබුල් රුක වීර පලු මොරද දුටු දනෝ
බුබුල් පෙල පතර පත් ගැඹුර නොදනෝ
තඹුල් සඳ සපිරි තිල් සලුව ඇබරුනෝ
කඹුල් වාන ඔය පසු කර ලදගනෝ PV

180 නෙකතුන් වෙර සලුව වටලා ඇන්ද පෙමා
මෙකතුන් තුරග මිනි නද නිතිවින්ද පෙමා
තකදොන් කුඹු ලෙලෙන විකරන් මෙන්ද ගැමා
දැකපන් මිතුර මේ වෙල හඳ පාන් ගමා PV

නෙකතුන් වෙර සුවඳ ලා ලා ලඳ සෑම
මෙකතුන් තුසර මුව දිසිදිළි කා රම
තකදොන් කුඹු ලෙලෙන විකසිත මෙන් සෑම
දැකපන් මිතුරෙ මන්වෙල හඳ මාන් ගම A1

dennā læya rana hansavi dura patara
ænna giyē pennā salasala godura
menna liyē dækapan kirilāgedara

Palugassǣva

68

වියෝ දුකින් යන කල රැකි රක්ෂා   ව

ලියෝ උනු උනුන් නැත කිසි විස්සා   ව

පයෝදර මනා කොඳ කොකු උස්සා   ව

ගියෝ යන්න පසු කර පලුගස්සෑ   ව

viyō dukin yana kala ræki rakṣāva

liyō unu unun næta kisi vissāva

payōdara manā koňda koku ussāva

giyō yanna pasukara palugassǣva

Moragashvǣva

69

කරඋස් නිල් දෙනෙත් යුග දඟසේ විර   ය

උරහිස් මුතු ඔහණ කැරකෙයි කා මලි   ය

පුර විස්තර අඟන යනමඟ රෑම ගි   ය

මොරගස්වැවත් පසුකර යනවාළු ලි   ය[181]

karaus nil denet yuga daňgasē viraya

urahis mutu m̆bahaṇa kærakeyi kā maliya

pura vistara aňgana yanamaňga rǣma giya

moragashvǣvat pasukara yanavāḷu liya

Mǣtiyakgama

70

වැටියක් වරල සිබිනිඳු කරණිලේ කො   ද

කැටියක් දෙකුඹු පිට ගෝඹර[182] දිලේ බ   ද

අටියක් රණ රතඹර අඟණෝළු සො   ද

---

[181] කර උස්සා දෙනෙත් යුඟ වෙස විය
නුර ඉස්සා මුව කැර කෙයි කාමලිය
පුර විස්තර අඟනක් නිති රුව ගිය
මොර ගස්වැව පසුකර යනවාලු ලිය PV

[182] ගෝඹර BL ගෝමර M1, M2

මැටියක්ගම ඇලෙන් ගියො ලඳ ලියෝ සො ද[183]

vǣṭiyak varala sikinindu karaṇilē koňḍa
kǣṭiyak dekum̌bu piṭa gōbara dilē baňḍa
aṭiyak raṇa ratam̌bara aňgaṇōḷu soňḍa
mǣṭiyakgama ǣlen giyō laňḍa liyō soňḍa

Nāgolla

71 රිලාවන් වඳුරු කොඳණඳ ලා ලොල් ල
කලාවුන් ලිහිනි සිකිනිඳු පැහැ නිල් ල
මුලාවෙන් සලෙළු මඟ යනවා ගොල් ල
බලාපන් නෝන නෑනේ නාගොල් ල[184]

rilāvan vaňduru koňḍaṇaňda lā lolla
kalāvun lihini sikinidu pæhæ nilla
mulāven saleḷu maňga yanavā golla
balāpan ṇōna nǣnē nāgolla

Karambē Pidivilla

72 රන් දැක ලඳගනෝ යුගදග සොම්පුල් ල
කන් දෙක සක් පතුර මේ වර සැරසිල් ල
උන් දැක සෙසු ලියෝ පරදිති සුන ගිල් ල
ගන් දෙක පසු කරපු කරබෙ පිදිවිල් ල

ran dæka laňdaganō yugadaga somipulla
kan dæka sak patura mē vara særasilla
undæka sesuliyō paraditi sunagilla

---

[183] වැටියක් වරල පිල්සිකි නිඳු තෙලේ කොඳ
කැටියක් දෙකුබු පෙතිගෝ'මර දිලේ බඳ
අටියක් කරන රක බර අගදන නොහොඳ
මැටියක් ගම ඇලෙන් යන ලඳ ලියෙන් සොඳ PV

[184] රිලාවන් වඳුරු කොක නඳ ලා ලොල්ල
කැලා උන් ලිහිනි සිකිනිඳු පැ නිල්ල
මුලා වෙන් සලෙළු මඟ යන වා ගොල්ල
බලා පන් ඔන්න නෑනේ නා ගොල්ල PV

gandeka pasu karapu karambē pidivilla

Dahanaggama

73

නෙත් පටු[185] නලල අඩ සඳ පියුමක් ලෙස   ට

සිත් තුම[186] දිගු යුවල ලෙල සළුවක් අත   ට

අත් දුටුවක් අඟන අඳුනක් නෙත්[187] කව   ට

විත් බටු ලියෝ ගොස් වෙති දහනග්ගම   ට[188]

net paṭu nalala aňda saňda piyumak lesaṭa

sittuma diňgu yuvala lela saḷuvak ataṭa

at duṭuvak aňgana aňdunak net kavaṭa

vit baṭuliyō gos veti dahanaggamaṭa

Niyadavanē

74

එබඳ වනේ[189] ගිරි සිරි ලෙන විපා ගෙ   ට

එමැද වනේ පස් ඇර රුව[190] විපා ගෙ   ට

රුවද වනේ දැක දුන්නෝ[191] අපාය   ට

නියදවනේ වැදලා ගිය[192] දෙපොය   ට

pabada vanē giri siri lena vipāgeṭa

emæda vanē pas æra ruva vipāgeṭa

ruvada vanē dæka dunṇō apāyaṭa

niyadavanē væňḍalā giya depōyaṭa

Potuvælpiṭiya

75

සම්ගම කලොත් යන ලඳ ලැජ්ජා හැටි   ය

රම්ගම සුරං කොමලඳ නුඹලා අටි   ය

---

185 ලටු PV

186 සිත්තුට BL සිත්තුටු M1, M2, සිතුතුටු PV

187 අඟන අඳුනන්තේ PV

188 දහනගමට BL දහනග්ගමට M1, M2 දැහැතක්ගමට PV

189 පබඳ මෙනේ PV

190 පස් ගැසුරුව PV

191 වැද නොය PV

192 නියද ගනේ වැදගෙන ගියේ PV

පෙම්දම සරං සර සඳ ලදලා අටි   ය

පිංගම නොහොත් හොඳගම පොතුවැල්පිටි   ය[193]

samgama kalot yana laňda læjjā hæṭiya

ramgama suran komalaňda num̆balā aṭiya

pamdama saran sara saňda ladalā aṭiya

pingama nohot hoňḍagama potuvælpiṭiya

Talpatgiri Kanda

76   රඟනත රැවු ගෝණ මුව වසු කරකු   න්ද

මේගන වග වලස් දිවිසිරි ලෙහෙනු   න්ද

ගඟගිරි මයුර කාවත[194] ලිහිනි   න්ද

නැගෙනහිර පෙණෙයි තල්පත්ගිරි ක   න්ද

raňganata rævu gōṇa muva vasu karakunda

mēghana vaga valas divisiri lehenunda

gaňgagiri mayura kāvāta lihininda

nægenahira peneyi talpatgiri kanda

Pāmihan Kanda

77   ජාති පින් කුසල් කළ ලඳ නියම ක   ර

නීතිහංකාර ලිය පිරිවරිණි බ   ර

ගීති කන්තීනි උණනුන් වරින් ව   ර

පාමිහං කන්ද බලසකි නැගෙණහි   ර

jāti pin kusal kaḷa laňda niyama kara

nītihankāra liya pirivariṇi bara

gīti kantīni uṇanun varin vara

pāmihan kanda balasaki nægeṇahira

---

[193] සන්ගම කලොත් යන ලඳ ලැජ්ජා කැටිය
රන්ගම සුරන් කොමලඳ නුඹලා දුටිය
පන්දම සරසලා ලඳ නුඹලා දුටිය
පින්ගම නොහොත් හොඳගම පොතුවැ පිටිය PV

[194] කාවාඩන M1, කාවාඹන M2

Yāpahu Kanda

78

මෙණෙයි දිළි සිරිනි සිරි සිළි කන් පිරි   ය

රණෙයි රුවන්[195] උරරැපු සුර මොක්දැරි   ය

පුරෙයි කියා ලඳ කුසලින් පිරී ගි   ය

පෙණෙයි බටහිරට යාපහු ගම් ගිරි   ය

meṇeyi diḷi sirini siri siḷi kan piriya

raṇeyi ruvan urarupu sura mok dæriya

pureyi kiyā laṅda kusalin pirī giya

peṇeyi baṭahiraṭa yāpahu gam giriya

Kattam̆bugama

79

පවර වල වසන වග වලසුං තර   ග

ඉවර රැක් ලෙහෙණ වඳුරණ ගුම් කුර   ග

කවරවල සිටින සිකිනිදු වන් එර   ග

අවරගිර පෙණෙයි කට්ටඹු ගම් ගිර   ග

pavara vala vasana vaga valasun taraṅga

ivara ruk lehena vaṅduraṇa gum kuraṅga

kavaravala siṭina sibinidu van eraṅga

avaragira peṇeyi kaṭṭam̆bu gam giraṅga

Mūnamola

80

මෙතුම් රැලි වත ලෙලෙන නදදුන් මහන වෙ   ල

කැදුම්[196] මුව සිරිසිර පදුමම් ශර මූණ ලො   ල

සැකදුම්[197] ගිගු මෙක හඬ දුං ගොස හඬ නල   ල

තකදොම් කිට දැකපන් ලඳ මුණමො   ල

metum ræli vata lelena nadadun mahana vela

kædum muva sirisira padumam śara mūṇa lola

sækadum gigu meka haṇḍa dun gosa haṅḍa nalala

---

195 රුවකින් M1 රුවකිනි M2

196 කැදුම් M1. M2 ශදුම් BL

197 සැකැදුම් M1, M2 ශකදුම් BL

takadom kiṭa dækapan laňda mūṇamola

Mī Oya

81

සුබ විස්තරින් රණ්සළු ඇඳලා ඉඟ ට

නැඹ උස්සඳ රැසින් තුනු බඳලා පුර ට

බඹ උස්යට ගමින් දළදී සේ රුව ට

අඹගස්වැවෙන් ගිය ලඳලා මී ඔය ට

suba vistarin raṇsaḷu æňḍalā iṅgaṭa

næmba ussaňda ræsin tunu mbaňḍalā puraṭa

bamba usyaṭa gamin daḷadī sē ruvaṭa

ambagasvæven giya laňdalā mī oyaṭa

Nāpāælla

82

රූප තැල්ල කර වට බැඳි මුතු තැල් ල

කීප ගොල්ල වන් සිකිනිඳු වර බෙල් ල

දීප එල්ල වුණු ලෙස ලා සොම් පුල් ල

නාපඇල්ල පසුකර ගිය ලඳ ගොල් ල[198]

rūpa tælla kara vaṭa bæňdi mutu tælla

kīpa golla van sikinidu vara bella

dīpa ella vuṇu lesa lā somipulla

nāpaælla pasukara giya laňda golla

ūrāpola

83

වාරූ ණොාව කරට සත්පොට මුතු බහ ණා

පීරා නිල් වරල බැඳිමල් සේ සොඹ ණා

තෝරා ලිය බුලත් කන කට රත පේ ණා

---

198 රූපතැල්ල කරවට බැඳි මුතු නිල්ල
කීම ගොල්ල වර කිසි නිඳු වර බෙල්ල
දීප ගොල්ල උණු ලෙස ලඳෙ සොම් පුල්ල
නාප තැල්ල පැත ගියෙ අඟනෝ ගොල්ල PV

උෟරාපොල ගමින් යන ලද අස මා ^{ක199}

vāru ṇova karaṭa satpoṭa mutu bahaṇa
pīrā nil varala bændimal sē somḃaṇa
tōrā liya bulat kana kaṭa rata pēṇa
ūrāpola gamin yana laṅda asamāṇa

Ramḃā Væva

84 වින්ද සිරි අඟන පින් පෙත් බබා නො   ව
ඇන්ද සඳ සපිරි දෙනුවන් බඹා ලො   ව
රන්ද පෙති යුවල රණහංස අඹා නො   ව
කින්ද මෙගම දැනගල්ලා රඹාවැ   ව²⁰⁰

vinda siri aṅgana pin pet babā nova
ænda saṅda sapiri denuvan bamḃā lova
randa peti yuvala raṇahansa amḃā nova
kinda megama dænagallā ramḃā væva

Dembataganpitiya

85 කවට කන් සරූප නොව සිත තැවු   ල්ලා
රුවට ලැමද පෙති ගෝමර බල   ල්ලා
එවට දිළි දිමුතු මිණිදැම් කැර   ල්ලා
දෙමටගම්පිටිය සකි මේ ගම බොල   ල්ලා²⁰¹

kavaṭa kan sarupa nova sita tævullā

---

¹⁹⁹ වාරා නොකර රට සත් පොට මුතු බාන
පීරා බැඳි වරල බැදිමල් සසො හාන
තෝරා ලිය බුලත් කන කොට රතු පාන
උරා පොල ගමෙන් යන ලද අය මාන PV

²⁰⁰ වින්ද සිටි අඟන පින් පෙත් නොබා සිව
ඇන්ද සඳ සපිරි දෙනුවන් බබා ලොව
රන්ද පෙති යුවල රනහස අඹා කව
කිම්ද මෙගම දැන ගල්ලා රඹැවැව PV

²⁰¹ කවට කම් සරූප නොව සිත තැවුල්ලා
රුවට ලැමද පෙති ගෝමර කැරැල්ලා
එමට දිසි දිමුතු වරලෙස සුනිල්ලා
දෙමට ගම් පියස මේකද බොලල්ලා PV

ruvaṭa læmada peti gōmara balallā
evaṭa diḷi dimutu minidam kærællā
demaṭaganpiṭiya saki mē gama bolallā

Galgiriyā Kanda

86 නෙලා මල් රහැණ වරලෙසලා බැ   න්ද[202]
වෙලා පට දුහුල් සිහිනිඟලා ඇ   න්ද
ලොලා බඹා[203] රණ හන්ස ලැම පිට නි   න්ද
බලාපන් නෑන ගල්කිරියා ක   න්ද

nelā mal ræhæṇa varalesalā bænda
velā paṭa duhul sihiniṅgalā ænda
lola bam̆bā raṇa hansa læma piṭa ninda
balāpan næna galkiriyā kanda

Galgiriyā Væva

87 කල් ඇරියා තොපි අපි පෙරසිට ඥා   න[204]
සිල් දැරියා කල කුසලින් අසමා   න
වල් ඇරියා ලෙස සන පිරිසිදු පා   න
ගල් කිරියා වැව දැකපන් මගෙ නෑ   න[205]

kal æriyā topi api perasiṭa gnāna
sil dæriyā kala kusalin asamāna
val æriyā lesa ghana pirisidu pāna
gal kiriyā væva dækapan mage næna

Boravæva

88 රන සපු සමන් දුනුකේ සුදු සේ   මා

---

202 ඇැන් ද PV

203 වඩත PV

204 Ending with ණ in all 4 lines BL

205 කල් ඇැරියා අපි තොපි පෙර සිට නෑන
සිල් දැරියා කලකුසලින් අසමාන
වල් ඇැරියා වැති කුසලට මග පාන
ගල් ගිරියා වැව නුඹදැකපන් නෑත PV

ගාන සඳුන් වෙර පිනිදිය රෙද්ද තෙ   මා

පාන කුඹු ලැමඳ පියයුරු දෙපල ලැ   මා

නෑන මේකවඳ බොරවෑව කියන ග   මා

ræna sapu saman dunuke sudu sēmā

gāna sandun vera pinidiya redda temā

pāna kumbu læmeda piyayuru depala læmā

næna mēkavada boravæva kiyana gamā

Talaaňḍapiṭiya

89   ලඳඹඳ ලැමඳ රණ හංෂ ගෝමර කැටි   ය

ෙකාඳ නඳ රෑණ වරලෙස ගවසා අටි   ය

අඳහස වීර රතිලිය සුරගණ වටි   ය[206]

ෙහාඳගම මේක පරසිඳු තලඅඳ පිටි   ය

laňdabaňda læmada raṇa hansa gōmara kæṭiya

koňda naňda ræṇa varalesa gavasā aṭiya

adahasa vīra ratiliya suraňgaṇa vaṭiya

hoňḍamagama mēka parasidu talaaňḍapiṭiya

Siyam̌balangomuva

90   ලියල්ලා වරල බැඳිමල් පිටිනි ෙකා   ඳ

වියපුලා වතුර බුබුලැති ගැඹුර න   ඳ

දිය සලා නලල මුතු රණ හංස ෙකා   ඳ

සියඹලංගොමුවේ ඔය පෑණ ගියා ල   ඳ[207]

liyallā varala bædimal piṭini koňḍa

viyapulā vatura bubulæti gæm̌bura naňḍa

diya salā nalala mutu raṇa hansha koňḍa

---

[206] අදහම් සුරලියන් සුරගා ලාවටිය PV

[207] ලියලා වරල දිදිගුමල් පටිනි ෙකාද
විස පුලා වතුර බුබුලැලි ගැඹුර කඳ
දිය සලා නානලඳ මුතු රතග හඳ
සියඹලාං ගමුවේ ඔය ගැන ගිෙයා් ලද PV

siyambalangomuve oya pæṇa giyā laṅḍa

Habaravatta

91 තඹර රත්න වඳ බඳ ලෙලණ වළු ල   මා
බඹර රොත්ත බිඟුකල රං රොණට න   මා[208]
දඟර පැත්ත වරලෙස ගවසාපු ල   මා[209]
හබරවත්ත පසු කර යනවාළු ල   මා[210]

tambara ratta vaṅḍa baṅḍa lelaṇa vaḷu lamā
bambara rotta biṅgukala ran roṇaṭa namā
daṅgara pætta varalesa gavasāpu lamā
habaravatta pasukara yanavāḷu lamā

Kaṅdulugamuva

92 තැල්ල මුතුමාල කරවට ලාන ගෙ   ලේ
ලොල්ල වඩන රන්බඳ දෙකුඹු මුතු පෙ   ලේ
දුල්ල දිව දුහුල් ඇඳි නෙරිය වන් ඇ   ලේ
ගොල්ල ලියෝ බැස යති කඳුලුගමු වෙ   ලේ

tælla mutumāla karavaṭa lāna gelē
lolla vaḍana ranbanda dekumbu mutu pelē
dulla diva duhul ændi neriya van ælē
golla liyō bæsa yati kaṅdulugamu velē

Kallanciya

93 සෙල්ලන් කලේ ලද නුඹ පල්ලා මිතු   ර
සෙල්ලන් [211]නොකර පින්කර පල්ලා පව   ර
තැල්ලෙන් මුවාකර ලැම රණහන්ස යතු   ර

---

[208] රොණට ලමා BL
[209] ගවසාපු පෙමා M1, M2
[210] තබර රත්න බඳ බැඳ ලෙල වාලු යොමා
බමර රොත්ත බිඟුකැල රන් රොනට හැමා
දහර පෙත්ත වර ලෙස ගවසාපු පෙමා
හබර වත්ත පසු කර යන වාලු ලමා PV
[211] ලෙල්ලන් M2, PV

කල්ලන්චියේ වෙල දැක පල්ලා මිතු· ර

sellan kalē laṅda numba pallā mitura
sellan nokara pinkara pallā pavara
tællen muvākara læma raṇahansa yatura
kallanciyē vela dæka pallā mitura

Nǣgama

94 රූපෙට අලන්කාරව ලිය කඹවුන්· නේ[212]
ආගම සළු පැලඳ රූබර ලියන්· නේ
ඒගම සිටින අඟනෝ ආගමකුත් නොදන්· නේ[213]
නෑගම වෙලේ සිටි අඟණෝ යොනුන්· නේ[214]

rūpeṭa alankārava liya kambavunnē
āgama saḷu pælaṅda rūbara liyannē
ēgama siṭina aṅgaṇō āgamakut nodannē
nǣgama velē siṭi aṅgaṇō yonunnē

95 දුල් පුල් මල් පියුම් පෙති බඳ මුතු බහ· ණ
මල් තැලි[215] දෙකුඹු මුතු ගෝමර පෙති සේ· ණ
නිල් පුල් මල් දෙනෙත් බෑම තුරු යුග පා· ණ
සල් පිල් වල සිටිණ යොන් ලිය අසමා· ණ

dul pul mal piyum peti baṅda mutu bahaṇa
mal tæli dekumbu mutu gōbara peti sēṇa
nil pul mal denet bæma turu yuga pāṇa
sal pil vala siṭiṇa yon liya asamāṇa

Niyangama

96 කොදෙල්ලා ඇමුණු මුතු ගෙල ලියන්ද· ම

---

[212] කොවුන්නේ PV

[213] ඒ ගම සිටින ආගම ඇත කතුන්නේ PV

[214] නෑගම වෙලේ සිටිනා ලද යොවුන් නේ PV

[215] මල් වැල් PV

බදෙල්ලා සළුව රතිලිය ලියං හෑ   ම

නදෙල්ලා වළළු යුග දඟ රුවන් ද   ම

ලදෙල්ලා ගියෝ පසුකර නියනඟ   ම[216]

koňdallā æmuṇu mutu gela liyandama

baňdallā saḷuva ritiliya liyan hæma

naňdallā vaḷaḷu yuga daňga ruvan dama

laňḍallā giyō pasukara niyangama

Valasvæva

97   පිය බඳ රත ලෑමඳ දිළි මුතු වෙණස් ණො   ව

රිය කොඳ සකි සමන් දිසි දිළි විලස් බ   ව

ලිය හොඳ කැකුළු කොඳ පෙති රහස් නො   ව

ගිය ලඳ පසුකරණ මහවෙල වළස්වෑ   ව[217]

piri baňḍa rata læmeňḍa diḷimutu veṇas ṇova

riya koňḍa saki saman disi diḷi vilas bava

liya noda kækuḷu koda peti rahas nova

giya laňḍa pasukaraṇa mahavela valasvæva

Avukana

98   රොදේ වරල පීරා මල් බැඳීම   ය

බදේ ඉසුනු පෙති ගෝමර කදීම   ය

ධජේ බැඳපු වෙනි ලඳ දිළි රිදීම   ය[218]

ලදේනෝ වඳු[219] අවුකොණ ගල් විහාර   ය

---

[216] කොඳ ලලා ඇමුනු දිදිලි ගෙල සියන් හෑමා
බඳ සලා සළුව නිතිරන් පටින් හෑමා
නඳ ලලා වළළු යුගදඟ රුවන් දමා
ලඳ බලා ගියෝ පසුකර නියන් ගමා PV

[217] පිය බඳ රන් ලෑමඳ දිලි මුතු වෙහෙස තොව
රිය කොඳ සක් සමන් දිසි දිළු විලස් බව
ලිය හඳ කොඳ කැකුළු පෙති තුරු රතැස් බව
ගිය ලඳ පසුකර මහවෙල වළස් වෑව PV

[218] දඳේ බැඳපුවා වැනි දිසි සිළුමය PV

[219] ලඳේ නමැඳු PV

rodē varala pīrā mal bændīmaya
baňde isuṇu peti gōmara kadīmaya
dhajē bæňḍapu veni laňda diḷi ridīmaya
ḷaňdenō vaňdu avukaṇa gal vihāraya

Kalā Oya

99

බලා වම දකුන යනමග ගෙවා ගි ය[220]

පුලා පැන් බුබුළ් රැලි නිල සෙදී ම ය[221]

ගලා ජල දුවන සැඩ රැල ඔයේ දි ය

කලා ඔයෙන් විත් බටු ලඳ ලියෝ ගි ය

balā vama dakuna yanamaga gevā giya
pulā pæn bubuḷu ræli nila sedī maya
galā jala duvana sæda ræla oyē diya
kalā oyen vit baṭu laňḍa giyō giya

Puliyamkulama

100

ලාපෙම වඩණ අඟනෝ සණ රං සේ ම

සාහිම කොකුම ලඳලා ගිය තුන් තල ම

ආගම කොමලඳුන් මග බසිමින් ඇළු ම

මේ ගම නෝන නෑනේ පුලියම්කුල ම[222]

lāpema vaḍaṇa aňgaṇō ghaṇa ran sēma
sāhima kokuma laňdalā giya tun talama
āgama komalaňdun maňga basimin æḷuma
mē gama ṇōna nǣnē puliyamkulama

Mayilan Perumāva

101   මුසුකර රසැතුරණ් පෙති ගණතා   ව

---

[220] ගෙවා ලිය PV

[221] පුලා පැන් බුබුල රැලි රැලි ඔයේ දිය PV

[222] ලාපෙම වඩන සලෙලුන්ගේ රින් දිලුම
ගා හිම කොකු වැලඳ පිනිදිය ගුම්තලම
ආගම කොමලඳුන් ගම බසිමින් ඇළම
මේ ගම ඔන්න නෑනෝ පුලියන් කුලම PV

අසුකර රං බඳට සළු ඇඳගණ පේ ව
එසුරණ සරණලා බැඳ යන සේනා ව
පසුකර ලඳ ගියෝ මයිලං පෙරුමා ව[223]

musukara rasæturaṇ peti gaṇanāva

asukara ran baṅḍaṭa saḷu æṅḍagaṇa pēva

esuraṇa saraṇalā bæṅḍa yana sēnāva

pasukara laṅḍa giyō mayilan perumāva

Mudaperumāgama

102 වැඩ කෙරුවා ලෙස සණ රන් අඟ ණ
තුඩ දැරුවා බිඹු පල මුව තඹර රො ණ
හඬ කෙරුවා ගීනදදී මිණි නදි ණ
මුඩපෙරුමාගම පසුකර යන අඟ ණ[224]

væḍa keruvā lesa ghaṇa ran aṅgaṇa

tuḍa dæruvā bim̆bu pala muva tam̆bara roṇa

haṅda keruvā gīnadadī miṇi nadiṇa

muḍaperumāgama pasukara yana aṅgaṇa

Ihalagama and Kāgama

103 පහළ වුනු කුසල් ලදලා ලමින් ගිවි ය
යහල ජල පතසේ අකුසල් දුරින් ගි ය
යුවල වත පැළඳ රං ලිය රෙණෙන් රි ය[225]
ඉහළගම පසුව කාගම ගමින් ගි ය[226]

---

[223] මුසුකර පවරලා නැඟ පෙති ගන්නාව
අසුකර රන්බඳට සලු ඇඳ ගන් පේව
පසුකර සරනලා වැඳ යන සේනාව
පසුකර ලද ගියෝ මයිලන් පෙරුමාව PV

[224] වැඩ කෙරුවා ලෙස දිදිලිරන් අඟනගන
තුඩ දරුවා බිගු පලමුව තබර රොන
හැඬ කෙරුවා ගියලඳ ලිය මීනි නදන
මුඩ පෙරුවා ගම පසුකර යන අඟන PV

[225] රෙණෙන් ලිය M2

[226] පහල වුනු කුසල් ලද ලා න මින් වීය

pahaḷa vunu kusal laṅdalā nalamin viya

yahala jala patasē akusal durin giya

yuvala vata pæleṅḍa ran liya raṇen riya

ihaḷagama pasuva kāgama gamin giya

Ratnāgala Halmilavǣva

104

ගන් පාබල පිරිවර අවිගන් කෝ   ක

යුත් රූපෙල සුරගණ මිස වෙන කෝ   ක

යොමුකර පියයුරන් ලියනද සෝ   ක

රත්නාගල හල්මිලවැව දෝ මේ   ක[227]

gan pābala pirivara avigan kōka

yut rūpela suraṅgaṇa misa vena kōka

yomukara piyayuran liyanada sōka

ratnāgala halmilavæva dō mēka

105

සැණකෙළි රිසි කෙළින වඳුරණ පැණ ගො   ල්ල

කැණහිල මුව ගෝනු මද ගජ තුරු නැ   ල්ල

මණ කල වග වලස් දිවි සිකිනිදු ගො   ල්ල

වනබල ගෙවා ගෙණ ගිය ලඳ සොම් පු   ල්ල[228]

sæṇakeḷi risi keḷina vaṅduraṇa pæṇa golla

kæṇahila muva gōnu mada gaja turu nælla

maṇa kala vaga valas divi sikinidu golla

vanabala gevā geṇa giya laṅda somipulla

ගලා යන දියසෙ අකුසල් දුරින් ගිය
දුහුල වන් පැලඳි රන්ලිය රනෙත ගිය
ඉහළ ගම පසුව ලඳ කාගමින් ගිය PV

[227] ගත් පාබල පිරිවර අවිගෙන නේක
යුත් රූපේ ල සුනු මිස වෙන කෝක
ගොත් වූ කලේ පියයුරු රති ලිය සෝක
රත්න ගල හල්මිල්ලෑ වද මේක PV

[228] සෑන කෙලි සිරි ලෙහෙන වදුරන් පන ගොල්ල
කැනහිල් මුව ගෝ කුලු මද ගජතැල්ල
මන කල් වගවලස් දිවි සිකිනිදු නිල්ල
වන වාහල ගෙවා ගියලද සොම් පුල්ල PV

ætavīra Væva

106

කළසකි කුඹු ලැමැද මුතු පෙති රැන මු   ව
දිලසකි එගම පිරි කෙළිනා කොළ යස   ව[229]
බෙදතිනි කීරලඳ ගණ රං රුව බල   ව
බලසකි මිතුරෙ දුටුවද ඇටවීර වැ   ව[230]

kaḷasaki kum̆bu læmæda mutu peti rēna mūva

dilasaki egama piri keḷinā koḷu yasava

bedatini kīralan̆da gaṇa ran ruva balava

balasaki miture duṭuvada æṭavīra væva

Nochchi Kulama

107

කච්චි සළු වැලද තුනු ඉඟ රූප සො   ඳ[231]
වෙච්චි වරද සතහට දුක් සෝක වු   ද
නිච්චි නැතුව පියයුරු ලෙල දේළු බ   ඳ
නොච්චිකුලම පසුකර යනවාළු ල   ඳ[232]

kachci saḷu vælada tunu iṅga rūpa son̆ḍa

vechci varada satahaṭa duk sōka vuda

nichci nætuva piyayuru lele dēḷu ban̆ḍa

nochcikulama pasukara yanavāḷu lan̆ḍa

Tōruvæva

108

ගෝරු හඳුන් තෙල් පිනිදිය ගා නා   න[233]
වාරු උනත් වරගණ අඟණෝ ද වෙ   න

---

[229] කෙළිනා නොව යසව M1

[230] කලසකි කුඹු ලැමැද මුතු පෙති නැර මුව
විලසකි එගම පිරි කෙළි කොලු රූම් හෙව
බොලදැති ටිකිරි ලඳ ගන රන් රූප හෙව
බල සකි මිමිතුර දුටුවද අටවීර වැව PV

[231] ඳ ending at every line M1, M2

[232] කච්චි සලුව ඇඳ තුනු ඉඟ රූසිර කඳ
වෙච්ච වරද හරිනට සිත් සෝක උද
නිච්චි නැතුව පියයුරු ලෙල වාපු බඳ
නොච්චි කුලම පසුකර යනවාළු ලඳ PV

[233] පිනි දිය ගඟා යන M1, M2

පිරු නෙළුන් වරලෙස ගවසා නය   න

තෝරුවැවත් පසුකර ලඳ ගනෝ ය   න

gōru haňdun tel pinidiya gā nāna
vāru unat varaṅgaṇa aňgaṇō da vena
pīru neḷun varalesa gavasā nayana
tōruvævat pasukara laňda gaṇō yana

Kaduruvǣgama

109 විදුරු දල මුවර රන් බිඹුල කාර   ව[234]

නුදුරු ලැමද පෙති ගෝමර ගෙතූ රූ   ව

සොඳුරු වරල මල් ගවසා ගෙතූ රූ   ව

කදුරුවැගමින් යන ලඳ අපූරූ   ව

viduru dala muvara ran biṁbula kārava
nuduru læmada peti gōmara getū ruva
soňduru varala mal gavasā getū ruva
kaduruvǣgamin yana laňda apūruva

Māminiyava

110 බඳේ පුලා රත්රණ තිසරුණේ ලැ   ය

දඳේ මෙලා ගෙන් ලෙල ලඳ ලියෝ ගි   ය

විසේ සලාපන් සඳ රැස කලා ග   ය

ලඳේ බලාපන් මාමිනියාවෙ ඔ   ය[235]

baňde pulā ratraṇa tisaruṇē læya
dade melā gen lela laňda liyō giya
visē salāpan saňda ræsa kalā gaya
laňdē balāpan māminiyave oya

---

[234] විදුරු ලද මුවර රති බිගුලා කරව PV

[235] බඳේ පුලා රන්රති සරැ පතේලය
දඳේ වෙලා ගෙන ලෙල ලඳ ලියෝ ගිය
වඳේ සලා පත් සරනද කාලගය
ලඳේ බලා පන් මාමිනි යාවෙ ඔය PV

Am̆batalē Vela

111 රැලේ වගවලස් මද ගජ පෙලේ පෙ ... ලේ
රැලේ රුක් ලෙහෙණ වඳුරණ වැලේ ර ... ලේ[236]
බලේ අදහගණ[237] සළු ඇඳ නිලේ නි ... ලේ
කැලේ ගෙවා ගණ බටු[238] අඹතලේ වෙ ... ලේ

rælē vagavalas mada gaja pelē pelē

rælē ruk leheṇa vaňduraṇa vælē rælē

balē adahaṅgaṇa saḷu æňḍa nilē nilē

kælē gevā gaṇa baṭu am̆batalē velē

Rīṭigala

112 වලාවන් ලගින ගිරි ශිරි තුරු කැ ... න්ද[239]
පුලා පැන් පොකුනු පලවැල විලිකු ... න්ද
නිලා[240] රුක් ලෙහෙණ දිවි වග වලසු ... න්ද
බලාපන් මිතුරෙ සිරි රිටිගල[241] ක ... න්ද[242]

valāvan lagina giri śiri turu kænda

pulā pæn pokunu palavæla vilikunda

nilā ruk leheṇa divi vaga valasunda

balāpan miture siri riṭigala kanda

Am̆batalē

113 කර ණිල්ලේ සිකිනිදු ගෙලෙහි දිළි නි ... ලේ
උර ණිල්ලේ මුතුරණ ඔහණ වර පෙ ... ලේ[243]

---

[236] වඳුරණ වැලේ වැලේ M1, ලොලේ දැක ලෙහෙන වඳුරන් රැලේ රැලේ PV

[237] අගන PV

[238] කැලේ ගෙවා ගොස් වනි PV

[239] ගිරි සිරි තුරු කැන්ද M1, වලාවන් නීල ගිරි තුසිරි තුරු කුන්ද PV

[240] රිලා PV

[241] මිතුරෙ සිට රිටි ගල් PV

[242] බලාපන් මිතුරු සිටි රිටිගල කන්ද BL

[243] කර නිල්ලේ සිකිනිදු ගෙලසෙ පිලි නිලේ
උර බෙල්ලේ රන්මුදු බාන ලැම තුලේ PV

සැර සිල්ලේ[244] පිනිදිය කොකුම වෙර පෙ   ලේ
පුරණල්ලේ හොඳගම මේක අඹත   ලේ

kara ṇillē sikinidu gelehi diḷi nilē
ura ṇillē muturaṇa m̐bahaṇa vara pelē
særa sillē pinidiya kokuma vera pelē
puraṇallē hoṅḍagama mēka am̐batalē

Kananpēdiyāgama

114   ගණන් වාඩි පසුකරලදෑ ලියෝ ගි   ය[245]
දනන්නාඩි තොර ණොව ඉදිරියේ ලි   ය
මෙනන් ජාඩි රස බෝජණ ලබා පු   ය
කනන්පේඩියාගම වනවල ගෙවා ගි   ය

ganan vādi pasukaraladæ liyō giya
danannāḍi tora ṇova idiriyē liya
menan jādi rasa bōjaṇa labā puya
kananpēdiyāgama vanvala gevā giya

Tōrankulama

115   සළු නිල්ලා පුරැ ලිය වරන් කළ තළ   ම
සොළුවැල්ලා ගව මුව ඌරං තල   ම
දේළු හඩ ගිගුං දිවි ගජයිං තල   ම
පාළගම මේක නම තෝරංකුල   ම

saḷu nillā puræ liya varan kaḷa taḷama
soḷuvællā gava muva ūran talama
dēḷu haḍha gigun divi gajayin talama
pāḷugama mēka nama tōrankulama

Kashtamurinchāna

116   ඉෂ්ට වෙන කුසල් පින් පෙත් ලා ලෝ   ක

---

[244] ශර සිල්ලෙ BL

[245] ගණන් වාඩි පසුකරලදැති යෝ ගිය BL

දුෂ්ට නපුරු සිත් එළවාලා අහ   ක

අෂ්ට අඟ සීලය රැකිදා ණය   ක

කෂ්ටමුරින්වානේ ගම දෝ මේ   ක[246]

iṣhṭa vena kusal pin pet lā lōka

duṣhṭa napuru sit elavālā ahaka

aṣhṭa aṅga sīlaya rækidā ṇayaka

kaṣhṭamurichcānē gama dō mēka

Soṅdavila

117   රූක ගුණ පළු වීර මොර රූක්ඕිද ලැවු   ව

කැක දුන් රැවුලෙ හෙණ කොකනද රණ හැඩු   ව

රැක වුන් ජල කිඹුළ බුබුලැති මුක තුඩු   ව

දැකපන් මිතුරෙ සොඳවිල මේ කටු මඩු   ව[247]

ruka guṇa paḷu vīra mora rukm̆biṅda lævuva

kæka dun rævule heṇa kokanada raṇa hæṅduva

ræka vun jala kim̆buḷu bubulæti muka tuduva

dækapan miture soṅdavila mē kaṭu maduva

Praising of Ulagalla's ancestral heritage

Ualagalla Væva

118   බටු බඳ ඔය ගෙවා ගණ වැද සිරිසි   ල්ල

කටු කොඳ පෙති ඇතුල තුල ලඳ දිලි තැ   ල්ල[248]

---

[246] ඉස්ට වන කුසල් පින් පෙත් ලා ලෙක
දුෂ්ට නපුරු සිත් ලෙල වාලා ලෝක
අස්ටාන්ගු සීලේ රැකිදා නේක
කස්ට මුරන් වානේ ගම වද මේක PV

[247] රැක තුන් පලු වීර මොර රැගු රුඉන් දුව
තකදොන් රැවුල් හෙත කොක නද රත අවුව
රැක බුන් ජල කිඹුල් බුබුලැලි මුක තුඩුව
දැකපන් මිතුර හොඳ විල කටුවේ මඩුව PV

[248] බටු ලඳ ඔබින්නේ මගොඩ වන සිරි සිල්ල
නටු කොඳ පෙති ඇමුනු ලැම තුල දිසිදිල්ල PV

බටු බඳ තුමුල් නිලඹර[249] සළු සැරසි   ල්ල
දුටුවද ලඳේ වැව පරසිදු උල ග   ල්ල

baṭu baṇḍa oya gevā gaṇa væda sirisilla

kaṭu koṇḍa peti ætula tula lada dili tælla

baṭu baṇḍa tumul nilaṁbara saḷu særasilla

duṭuvada laṅdē væva parasidu ulagalla

119
නිල්ල ජල රැල්ල පිරි සුදු නැලවි   ල්ල
වැල්ල සිසි ලැල්ල රතඹර ඔළ ගො   ල්ල
ලොල්ල සොම්පුල්ල ඔපලඳ කොඳ නි   ල්ල
දුල්ල පුරණල්ල පරසිදු උලග   ල්ල[250]

nilla jala rælla pirisidu nælavilla

vælla sisi lælla rataṁbara oḷu golla

lolla somipulla m̆bapalaṅda koda nilla

dulla puraṇalla parasidu ulagalla

Ulagalla Heritage and Kaḷu Kumara Mansion

120
දෙල් හල් අඹ දෙළුන් නාරං දොඩන් යු   තු
නිල්වැල් මල් කමල් නාසපු පොතන් අ   තු
මල් රැල් කිතුල් වද ඉඟු රැලින් ගෙ   තු
තල් පොල් තලතලා පුවකුඳු උයන් ව   තු

Del hal aṁba deḷun nāran doḍan yutu

nilvæl mal kamal nāsapu potan atu

mal ræl kitul vada ingu rælin getu

tal pol talatalā puvakudu uyan vatu

121
කාවල් මුර ජාම වට බර ඇඳ පතු   රැ
තුමල් වට පන්ති මුර ඇරකර ඉතු   රැ

---

[249] නිල් සර PV

[250] නිල්ල ජල රැල්ල සිරි සුදු නැලවිල්ල
වැල්ලා සිසි රැල්ල සිරි සුදු නැවිල්ල
ලොල්ලා සොම් පුල්ල උපුලඳ කොනිල්ල
දුල්ලා පුරනල්ල පරසිදු උල ගල්ල PV

විපුල් ගජ තුරග රිය පාබල මිතු රැ
පෙනේ බිම් මහල් උළු ගබඩා යතු රැ[251]

kāval mura jāma vaṭa bara æṅda paturu
tumal vaṭa panti mura ærakara ituru
vipul gaja turaṅga riya pābala mituru
penē bim mahal uḷu gabadā yaturu

122   කලඟ වෙඩි කවසි කගපත් ලැබුනු තැ ණ
        විලඟු වලළු බුවනෙක නිරිඳු ගෙන් දු ණ
        වලඟු රට තොට කඳු කඩවත් ලැබු ණ
        ඉලඟසිංහ කළු කුමරුගෙ මේ විම ණ[252]

kalaṅga vedi kavasi kagapat lebunu tæṇa
vilangu valaḷu buvaṇeka niridu gen duṇa
valangu raṭa toṭa kaṅdu kaḍavat læbuṇa
ilaṅgasinghe kaḷu kumaruge mē vimaṇa

Praising the remaining landmarks on the route

Mārākulama

123   සාර සඳ කැළුම මුව සිසිරාවන් හම න
        මෝරා කුඹු ලැමඳ පීණන හඳුං මෙ න
        තෝරා ලිය බුලත් කන කට රත දිලෙ න
        මාරාකුලම පසු කරමිං ඔයින් ය න[253]

---

[251] කාවල් මුර ජාම වට බැඳ ඇඳි යතුරු
තුමුල් වට පත්තිනි මුර ආකර ඉතුරු
විදුල් ගජතුරග රිය බාබල මිතුරු
ගෙවල් බින් වහල් උළු ගබඩා යතුරු PV

[252] කලංගු වෙඩි කවඩි කසසැර ලැබු තැන
විලංගු වළලු ලැබ බුවනෙක නිරිඳු ගෙන
වලංගු රටතොට කඳු කඩවත් බැගින
ඉලංග සිංහ කුල කුමරුගේ මේ විමන PV

[253] සාර සඳ කැළුම මුව සිසිර වන මෙනේ
මෝරා කුඹු ලැමඳ පිටතට නැග ශසුනේ
නෑරා පෙති කුසුම් බඳ මල් කැලුන් රොනේ
වාරා කුලම පසු කරමින් ඔයෙන් පැනේ PV

sāra saṅḍa kæḷuma muva sisirāvan hamana
mōra kum̆bu læmæda pīṇana haṅdun mena
tōrā liya bulat kana kaṭa rata dilena
mārākulama pasu karamin oyin yana

Uṭṭimaduva

124 වේට්ටි පට දුහුල් සිහිනිඟ සළුව හැ ද

 කට්ටි ලේ පරති කෙළි නොකරවුව ල ද

 කුට්ටි කර කනක මුතු ලෙල දේළු ඔ ද

 උට්ටිමඩුව පසුකර යනවාළ ල ද[254]

veṭṭi pata duhul sihiniṅga saḷuva hæṅḍa
kaṭṭi lē parati keḷi nokaravuva laṅḍa
kuṭṭi kara kanaka mutu lela dēḷu oṅḍa
uṭṭimaduva pasukara vanavāḷu laṅḍa

Orukkumān Kulama

125 මුරුක්කු රංමාල ගෙලෙ මුතුලා ඔහ න

 පෙරුක්කු කල පෙරටුව ගෝසා කර න

 කරුක්කු සොරණැ කුඩ කොඩි පෙළන දි න

 ඔරුක්කුමාන් කුලමට බැසපු එ අඟ න[255]

murukku ranmāla gele mutu lā m̆bahana
perukku kala peraṭuva gōsā karana
karukku soraṇæ kuḍa kodi peḷana dina
orukkumān kulamaṭa bæsapu ē aṅgana

---

[254] වේට්ටි පට දුහුල් සිහිනිඟ සළු ඇන්ද
 කාට්ටි ලේ පසුව යන අගනො'ලු සොඳ
 කට්ටි කරන කත මුතු ලෙල වාලු බඳ
 උාට්ටි කුලම පසුකර යනවාලු ලද PV

[255] මුරැක්කු රන්මාල ගෙලෙ මුතු ලාබරන
 පෙරෙක්කු කල පෙරටුව පස තුරු ගෙන
 කරුක්කු සුදු රතු මුතු කුඩ කොඩි ජේන
 ඔරුක්කවා කුලමට බැසපුව අගන PV

Venerating Gatulāgan Vihāre

126 නිල් ධජ කොත් යටඟ කිකිනද ගෝසා   ර

පුල්පෙති මල් තොරං රන් දිසි දිළි විදූ   ර

සල් සපු මල් වියන් ජවනික තිතිර සොඳූ   ර

කල් නොයවා බෑස වඳු පස් ඇස මදූ   ර[256]

nil dhaja kot yaṭaṅga kikinada gōsāra

pulpeti mal toran ran disi diḷi vidura

sal sapu mal viyan javanika titira soṅdura

kal noyavā bæsa vaṅdu pas æsa madura

127 රන්දන් නිල් පලස් ධජ මිනි කන්ගා   පු

ඇත්දත් සඳ කැළුම මුතු කොඩි නන්ගා   පු

කුන්දන් ගජඟ ගිඟු මෙන් හඬ තලා   පු

පන්දන් වැට උඩිං නිල්කොඩි නගා   පු[257]

randan nil palas dhaja mini kangāpu

ætdat saṅda kæḷuma mutukodi nangāpu

kundan gajaṅga gingu men haṅda talāpu

pandan væṭa udin nil kodi nagāpu

128 රස බදු සුගම් දම් සස ගුණ ප්‍රහා   රේ

වසවතු යුදය මරුවන් බිඳිමිං පා   රේ

ඉස ඉඳුවර කුසල් කළ ලඳ මුදා   රේ

බෑස වඳූ ලඳේ ගැටුලාගම් විහා   රේ

rasa badu sugam dam saṅga guṇa prabhāre

vasavatu yudaya maruvan biṅdimin pāre

isa iṅduvara kusal kaḷa laṅda mudāre

bæsa vaṅdu laṅde gaṭulāgan vihāre

---

[256] නිල් දද කොත් යටඟ බන් කිනි මිනි යතුර
පුල්පෙති මල් තොරන් සේසත් මිනි යතුර
සල්සපු මල් වියන් පවනිකා යෙන් සොදුර
කල් නොයවා බෑස වැදූ පස් ඇස මැදුර PV

[257] රන්දන් නිල් පලස් දදමිනි නගාපු
අන්දන් මිනි කැකුළු දිදිසි මුදු සලාපු
කුන්දන් ගජතුරග ගුම් හඩ නගාපු
පන්දන් වැට උඩින් නිල්කොඩි නගාපු PV

129
සෙනා දිදී එන සෙනගන් නොඹා ඇ දු[258]
පිනා සසර සාගරයන් ගෙවා යෙ දු
නානා මේ යුදයදී මුදුනත් තබා ඉ දු
නුනා පැලඳි සළු මුදුනත් තබා ව දු

sena didī ena senagan noṁbā æňdu

pīna sasara sāgarayan gevā yedu

nānā mē yudayedī mudunat tabā iňdu

nunā palaňdi saḷu mudunat tabā vaňdu

Presenting of Sandēśaya

130
මවා නික සිතින් එළු පද පතල ක ර[259]
පෑවා සේක බුවණෙක අදහසින් ක ර
පාවා දීපු රට තොට පට පහස් ක ර
බෝවා ආසිරින් මා නිදහසක් ක ර

mavā nika sitin eḷu pada patala kara

pǣvā sēka buvaṇeka adahasin kara

pāvā dīpu raṭa toṭa paṭa pahas kara

bōvā āsirin mā nidahasak kara

131
නරනිඳු බුවණෙක[260] යන නම නිරිඳු වෙ ත
පුර ඉඳු සඳ සිසිර ගොත් කැළමෙන් දිමු ත
සුරණිඳු කරුණු කුළනින් රට දෙවු වෙ ත
පරසිදු උලගල්ලේ මැතිඳුට වේය සෙ ත

naraṇidu buvaṇēka yana nama niriňdu veta

pura iňdu saňda sisira got kæḷumen dimuta

suraṇiňdu karuṇu kuḷunin raṭa devu veta

parasidu ulagalle metuduṭa vēya seta

---

[258] නොඹා ඉදු M1

[259] මවා නික සිතින් එළු පද පතල කර (NM 2175 catalogue entry) මවා නික සිතින් එළු පුද පවර කර BL, M1, M2

[260] බුවණේක BL

Appendix 1

Distribution of Stanzas among Manuscripts and Overlap

Contents of manuscripts

BL   There are 27 text pages in this manuscript with each side containing four quatrains making a total of 108 (27x4) verses. The numbering system includes the following. The first text page of the leaf has been referred to as 1a and the back page of the same leaf as 1b in this publication. The first verse of the fist page has been referred to as 1a.1 and the first verse of the back page of the same leaf as 1b.1 etc.

M1   There are 18 text pages in this manuscript with each ola-leaf page containing six verses which add up to 108 (18 x 6) verses. It has been referred to as 1.1 to the first verse on the first page and 1.6 to the last verse on the first page in this publication and six verses have been sighted here.

M2   There are 18 text pages in this manuscript with each ola-leaf page containing 6 verses which add up to 108 (18 x 6) verses. It has been referred to as 1.1 to the first verse on the first page and 1.6 to the last verse on the first page in this publication and six verses have been sighted here.

PV   There are 83 verses in this manuscript. The verses have been numbered in this publication as PV 1 to PV 83.

A1   There are 58 stanzas that are relevant to Aṣhtanārī Sandēśaya in this manuscript. The stanzas are listed in this publication as A1.1 and A1.2 etc.

Distribution of verses among manuscripts

#	BL	M1	M2	PV	A1

Launching the Sandēśaya and Celebrating the poet

#	BL	M1	M2	PV	A1
1	BL 1a.1	M1 1.1	M2 1.1		
2	BL 1a.2	M1 1.2	M2 1.2		
3	BL 1a.3	M1 1.3	M2 1.3		
4	BL 1a.4	M1 1.4	M2 1.4		

Praising the beauty of eight damsels (Dūta)

#	BL	M1	M2	PV	A1
5	BL 1b.1	M1 1.5	M2 1.5	PV 1	
6	BL 1b.2.	M1 1.6	M2 1.6		
7	BL 1b.3	M1 2.1	M2 2.1		
8	BL 1b.4.	M1 2.2	M2 2.2		A1 6
9	BL 2a.1.	M1 2.3	M2 2.3		A1 7
10	BL 2a.2	M1 2.4	M2 2.4	PV 2	A1 8
11	BL 2a.3	M1 2.5	M2 2.5	PV 3	A1 9
12	BL 2a.4	M1 2.6	M2 2.6		A1 10
13	BL 2b.1	M1 3.1	M2 3.1	PV 4	A1 11
14	BL 2b.2	M1 3.2	M2 3.2		A1 12
15	BL 2b.3	M1 3.3	M2 3.3	PV 5	A1 13
16	BL 2b.4	M1 3.4	M2 3.4	PV 6	A1 14
17	BL 3a.1	M1 3.5	M2 3.5	PV 7	A1 15

Praising of landmarks on the route
Samanola Kanda (Adams Peak)

#	BL	M1	M2	PV	A1
18	BL 3a. 2	M1 3.6	M2 3.6	PV 8	A1 20

Mīgahakum̐bura

#	BL	M1	M2	PV	A1
19	BL 3a.3	M1 4.1	M2 4.1	PV 9	A1 21

Uyanvatta

#	BL	M1	M2	PV	A1
20	BL 3a.4	M1 4.2	M2 4.2	PV 10	A1 22

Valpola

21	BL 3b.1	M1 4.3	M2 4.3	PV 11	A1 23
Kadavata Kælē					
22	BL 3b.2	M1 4.4	M2 4.4	PV 12	A1 24
Kollægala					
23	BL 3b.3	M1 4.5	M2 4.5	PV 13	A1 25
24					A1 26
25					A1 27
Batupiṭigama					
26	BL 3b.4	M1 4.6	M2 4.6	PV 14	A1 28
Randenivæla					
27	BL 4a.1	M1 5.1	M2 5.1	PV 15	A1 29
28	BL 4a.2	M1 5.2	M2 5.2	PV 16	
Yakdessā Kanda					
29	BL 4a.3	M1 5.3	M2 5.3	PV 17	A1 30
30					A1 31
Doḷu Kanda					
31	BL 4a.4	M1 5.4	M2 5.4	PV 18	A1 32
32					A1 33
Dunupataṅga					
33	BL 4b.1	M1 5.5	M2 5.5	PV 19	A1 34
Vallāgala					
34	BL 4b.2	M1 5.6	M2 5.6	PV 20	A1 35
35	BL 4b.3	M1 6.1	M2 6.1		A1 36
36					A1 37
37					A1 38
Mudannāpola					
38	BL 4b.4	M1 6.2	M2 6.2		A1 39
39	BL 5a.1	M1 6.3	M2 6.3		A1 40
40	BL 5a.2	M1 6.4	M2 6.4		A1 41
41	BL 5a.3	M1 6.5	M2 6.5		A1 42
42	BL 5a.4	M1 6.6	Sand 6.6		A1 43
Māṅguru Oya					
43	BL 5b.1	M1 7.1	M2 7.1	PV 21	A1 44
Aḷupotagan Væla					
44	BL 5b.2	M1 7.2	M2 7.2	PV 22	A1 45

45					A1 46
46					A1 47
47					A1 48

Vilgandemata Væva

| 48 | BL 5b.3 | M1 7.3 | M2 7.3 | PV 23 | A1 49 |

Balaḷuvāgāra

| 49 | BL 5b.4 | M1 7.4 | M2 7.4 | PV 24 | A1 50 |

Tissō Væla

| 50 | BL 6a.1 | M1 7.5 | M2 7.5 | PV 25 | A1 51 |

Yongama

| 51 | | | | | A1 52 |

Sērugolla

| 52 | BL 6a.2 | M1 7.6 | M2 7.6 | PV 26 | A1 53 |
| 53 | | | | | A1 54 |

Nuvara Kanda

| 54 | BL 6a.3 | M1 8.1 | M2 8.1 | PV 27 | A1 55 |
| 55 | | | | | A1 56 |

Dæduru Oya

56	BL 6a.4	M1 8.2	M2 8.2	PV 28	A1 57
57					A1 58
58					A1 59

Nindagama

| 59 | BL 6b.1 | M1 8.3 | M2 8.3 | PV 29 | A1 60 |
| 60 | | | | | A1 61 |

Divulvæva

61	BL 6b.2	M1 8.4	M2 8.4	PV 30	A1 62
62					A1 63
63					A1 64
64					A1 65

Kimbulvāna Oya

| 65 | BL 6b.3 | M1 8.5 | M2 8.5 | PV 31 | A1 66 |

Handapāngama

| 66 | BL 6b.4 | M1 8.6 | M2 8.6 | PV 32 | A1 67 |

Kirilāgedara

| 67 | | | | PV 33 | |

Palugassæva				
68				PV 34
Moragashvæva				
69	BL 7a.1	M1 9.1	M2 9.1	PV 35
Mætiyakgama				
70	BL 7a.2	M1 9.2	M2 9.2	PV 36
Nāgolla				
71	BL 7a.3	M1 9.3	M2 9.3	PV 37
Karambē Pidivilla				
72				PV 38
Dahanaggama				
73	BL 7a.4	M1 9.4	M2 9.4	PV 39
Niyadavanē				
74	BL 7b.1	M1 9.5	M2 9.5	PV 40
Potuvælpiṭiya				
75	BL 7b.2	M1 9.6	M2 9.6	PV 41
Talpatgiri Kanda				
76	BL 7b.3	M1 10.1	M2 10.1	
Pāmihan Kanda				
77	BL 7b.4	M1 10.2	M2 10.2	
Yāpahu Kanda				
78	BL 8a.1	M1 10.3	M2 10.3	
Kattambugama				
79	BL 8a.2	M1 10.4	M2 10.4	
Mūnamola				
80	BL 8a.3	M1 10.5	M2 10.5	
Mī Oya				
81	BL 8a.4	M1 10.6	M2 10.6	
Nāpāælla				
82	BL 8b.1	M1 11.1	M2 11.1	PV 42
Urāpola				
83	BL 8b.2	M1 11.2	M2 11.2	PV 43
Rambā Væva				
84	BL 8b.3	M1 11.3	M2 11.3	PV 44
Dembataganpitiya				

85	BL 8b.4	M1 11.4	M2 11.4	PV 45
	Galkiriyā Kanda			
86	BL 9a.1	M1 11.5	M2 11.5	PV 46
	Galkiriyā Væva			
87	BL 9a.2	M1 11.6	M2 11.6	PV 47
	Boravæva			
88				PV 48
	Talaañḍapiṭiya			
89	BL 9a.3	M1 12.1	M2 12.1	PV 49
	Siyam̌balangomuva			
90	BL 9a.4	M1 12.2	M2 12.2	PV 50
	Habaravatta			
91	BL 9b.1	M1 12.3	M2 12.3	PV 51
	Kaňdulugamuva			
92				PV 52
	Kallanciya			
93	BL 9b.2	M1 12.4	M2 12.4	PV 53
	Nǣgama			
94	BL 9b.3	M1 12.5	M2 12.5	PV 54
95	BL 9b.4	M1 12.6	M2 12.6	PV 55
	Niyangama			
96	BL 10a.1	M1 13.1	M2 13.1	BPV 56
	Valasvæva			
97	BL 10a.2	M1 13.2	M2 13.2	PV 57
	Avukana			
98	BL 10a.3	M1 13.3	M2 13.3	PV 58
	Kalā Oya			
99	BL 10a.4	M1 13.4	M2 13.4	PV 59
	Puliyankulama			
100	BL 10b.1	M1 13.5	M2 13.5	PV 60
	Mayilan Perumāva			
101	BL 10b.2	M1 13.6	M2 13.6	PV 61
	Mudaperumāgama			
102	BL 10b.3	M1 14.1	M2 14.1	PV 62
	Ihalagama and Kāgama			

103	BL 10b.4	M1 14.2	M2 14.2	PV 63

Ratnāgala Halmilavæva

104	BL 11a.1	M1 14.3	M2 14.)	PV 64
105	BL 11a.2	M1 14.4	M2 14.4	PV 65

Etavīra Væva

106	BL 11a.3	M1 14.5	M2 14.5	PV 66

Nochchi Kulama

107	BL 11a.4	M1 14.6	M2 14.6	PV 67

Tōruvæva

108	BL 11b.1	M1 15.1	M2 15.1	

Kaduruvǣgama

109	BL 11b.2	M1 15.2	M2 15.2	PV 68

Māminiyava

110	BL 11b.3	M1 15.3	M2 15.3	PV 69

Am̆batalē Vela

111	BL 11b.4	M1 15.4	M2 15.4	PV 70

Riṭigala

112	BL 12a.1	M1 15.5	M2 15.5	PV 71

Am̆batalē

113	BL 12a.2	M1 15.6	M2 15.6	PV 72

Kananpēdiyāgama

114	BL 12a.3	M1 16.1	M2 16.1	

Tōrankulama

115	BL 12a.4	M1 16.2	M1 16.2	

Kashtamurichchāna

116	BL 12b.1	M1 16.3	M2 16.3	PV 73

Soṅdavila

117	BL 12b.2	M1 16.4	M2 16.4	PV 74

Praising of Ulagalla's ancestral heritage

Ualagalla Væva

118	BL 12b.3	M1 16.5	M2 16.5	PV 75
119	BL 12b.4	M1 16.6	M2 16.6	PV 76

Ulagalla Heritage and Kaḷu Kumara Mansion

120	BL 13a.1	M1 17.1	M2 17.1	
121	BL 13a.2	M1 17.2	M2 17.2	PV 77

122	BL 13a.3	M1 17.3	M2 17.3	PV 78

Praising the remaining landmarks on the route
Mārākulama

123	BL 13a.4	M1 17.4	M2 17.4	PV 79

Uṭṭimaduva

124	BL 13b.1	M1 17.5	M2 17.5	PV 80

Orukkumān Kulama

125	BL 13b.2	M1 17.6	M2 17.6	PV 81

Venerating Gatulāgan Vihāre

126	BL 13b.3	M1 18.1	M2 18.1	PV 82
127	BL 13b.4	M1 18.2	M2 18.2	PV 83
128	BL 14a.1	M1 18.3	M2 18.3	
127	BL 13b.4	M1 18.2	M2 18.2	PV 83
128	BL 14a.1	M1 18.3	M2 18.3	
129	BL 14a.2	M1 18.4	M2 18.4	

Presenting of Sandēśaya

130	BL 14a.3	M1 18.5	M2 18.5	
131	BL 14a.4	M1 18.6	M2 18.6	

Appendix 2
System of Transliteration

අ	a	ඨ	ṭha
ආ	ā	ඩ	ḍa
ඇ	æ	ඪ	ḍha
ඈ	ǣ	ණ	ṇa
ඉ	i	ඬ	ňḍa
ඊ	ī	ත	ta
උ	u	ථ	tha
ඌ	ū	ද	da
ඍ	ṛ	ධ	dha
ඎ	ṝ	න	na
එ	e	ඳ	ňda
ඒ	ē	ප	pa
ඓ	ai	ඵ	pha
ඔ	o	බ	ba
ඕ	ō	භ	bha
ඖ	au	ම	ma
ක	ka	ඹ	m̌ba
ඛ	kha	ය	ya
ග	ga	ර	ra
ඝ	gha	ල	la
ඞ	ṅa	ව	va
ච	ca	ළ	ḷa
ඡ	cha	ශ	śa
ජ	ja	ෂ	ṣa
ඣ	jha	ස	sa
ඤ	ña	හ	ha
ට	ṭa	ෆ	fa

Appendix 3:
Bibliography and References

Andirishāmi, HB. (1909) Nārisath Sandēśaya, Kandy.

Appuhāmy, M D Dāmpi. (1909) Aṣhtanārī Sandēśaya. Sanka Magazinee. 2004. January-June Volume. Cultural Affairs Department. Colombo.

Arangala, Rathnasiri. (2021). Athpiyapathvala panena lekak dosha ha mulapata sanskaranayedi patanthara dakvime vadagathkama. 11 - 03 Volume, ISSN 2279-2020. Jathika Pusthakala ha Pralekana Seva Mandalaya.

Bandaranayake, B. (2021). South Indian Brāhmins in Sri Lankan Culture: Assimilation in Sath Korale & Kandyan Regions. Melbourne, Australia.

Bandaranayake, Bandara. (2022). Immigrants from Madurapura: A Collection of Ola-leaf Manuscripts in Sri Lanka. Melbourne, Australia.

Chaturvedi, BM, (1996). Some unexplained aspects of Rasa Theory. Vidyanidhi Prakashan. New Dilli.

D'Oyly, L (1995) Diary of Mr John D'Oyly, 1810-1815. Lake House Bookshop. Colombo.

Danansuriya, J. (200s). Sinhala Padya Sahithya – Mahanuwara Yugaye sita Dahanawawana Siyawase aga bagaya dakva. Kurunegala Sasthriya Sandrahaya. Part 2. Provincial Council North-Western.

Davy, J (1821) An Account of the Interior of Ceylon and its Inhabitants. London.

De Silva, W A (1927). Sinhalese Vittipot (books of events) and Kadayimpot (books of division boundaries). The Journal of the Ceylon Branch of the Royal Asiatic Society of Great Britain & Ireland, 1927, Vol. 30, No. 80, Parts I, II, III and IV. (1927), pp. 303-325 http://www.jstor.com/stable/43483797

De Silva, W. A (1938). Catalogue of Palm Leaf Manuscripts. Vol 1. Memoirs of the Colombo Museum. Series A No 4. Ceylon Government Press. Colombo.

De Silva, W. A. (1927) Sinhalease Viththi pot (books of Incidents) and Kadaimpot (Books Division Boundaries). The Journal of the Ceylon Branch of the Royal Asiatic Society of Great Britain & Ireland , Vol. 30, No. 80, Parts I, II, III and IV. pp. 303-325

Dharmasena Bandara Y M. (2011) Mahasammatha Vitti Book, in Nikawa Gampaha Aththayen Bindak.

Disanayake, Ilangasinghe M. (2007). Pothuwe Wel Vidane.

Ferguson, John. (1893) "Ceylon in 1893: Progress of the Island since 1803". Observer Press. Colombo.

Ghosh, Manomohan (2002). Natyasastra. ISBN 81-7080-076-5.

Godakumbura C.E. (1955). Sinhalese Literature, Colombo

Godakumbura, C E eds (1953). Hansa Sandēśaya. Colombo

Gonda, Jan. (1984). A History of Indian Literature. Vol 3. Wiesbaden.

Haksar, A.N.D. (1995) Glimps of Sanskrit Literature. Indian Council of Cultural Relations.

https://web.archive.org/web/20070212060836/http://www.parashakthitemple.org/pages/ashta_lakshmi.aspx

https://www.dinamina.lk/2021/03/30/Baratha ganithaya

https://www.wikipedia.org/

Indrapala K. (1969). Early Tamil Settlements in Ceylon. The Journal of the Ceylon Branch of the Royal Asiatic Society of Great Britain & Ireland, 1969, New Series, Vol. 13 (1969), pp. 43-63.https://www.jstor.org/stable/43483465.

Indrapala, K. (1970). The origin of the Tamil Vanni chieftains of Ceylon. Journal of the Humanities, July 1970, Vol 1, No 2 ISSN 2279-2120

Jayasekara, Mala Wasanthi. (218). Kotte Yugaye Sandesha Kavya ha Thotagamuve Sri Rahula. Godage Brothers, Colombo.

Karunananda, U B. (2005). Nuvarakalāviya, 1815-1900, S Godage Brothers. Colombo.

Kumaraswami, Ananda. (1932). Myths of Hidus and Buddhists. George G Harrap. London.

Kuruwita, Rangana. (2022). Ithibiso Jathakaya ha Ithibiso Jathaka Kawya, Surya Prakashakayo. Colombo.

Kuruwita, Rangana. (2015). Kurunegala Vistharaya, Surya Prakashakayo. Colombo

Macdonell, A. (1900). A history of Sanskrit Literature. New York

Marambe, A J W. (1926). Thrisinhale Kadayim saha Viththi. Lankadeepa Printers, Kandy.

Marchand, Peter The Yoga of the Nine Emotions: The Tantric Practice of Rasa Sadhana Paperback – Illustrated, 21 April 2006

Modder, F (1893), Kurunegala Wistharaya with Notes on Kurunegala ancient and Modern, No. 44 Journal of Royal Asiatic Society (Ceylon) Vol XIII

Moratuvagama, HM. (1997). Sinhala Sandesha Kavya. Godage Brothers, Colombo.

Nanayakkara, Kaveesha (2019) The importance and value of 'Sandesha Kāvya' in Sri Lanka. URI: http://repository.kln.ac.lk/handle/123456789/22984

Nevill, Hugh. (1955). Sinhala Verse Part 3. Colombo.

Obeyesekere, Gananath (2016). Caste Conflicts and Discourses during the Kandyan Kingdom: evidence from the Matale District. Keynote Speech 19 November 2016. International Centre for Ethnic Studies.

Obeyesekere, Gananath (ed. 2005) Vanni Upatha, Vanni Vitti and Vanni Kadayim potha, S Godage & Brothers.

Obeyesekere, Gananath (ed. 2005). Bandarawali and Kadayim Poth, S Godage & Brothers.

Obeyesekere, Gananath (ed. 2005). Malala Viththiya, Malala Kathawa saha Rajasinghe Rajuge Pruthigisi Satan Pilibandawa sandahan Vitti book, S Godage & Brothers

Obeyesekere, Gananath (ed. 2005). Vanni Rajawaliya, S Godage & Brothers.

Obeyesekere, Gananath. (1984).. The Cult of the Goddess Pattini. University of Chicago.

Obeyesekere, Gananath. (2004). The Matrilineal East Coast Circa 1968: Nostalgia and Post Nostalgia in Our Troubled Time. Speech on 2004 July

Obeyesekere, Gananath. (2013). The Coming of Brāhmins Migrants: The Śudra Fate of an Indian Elite in Sri Lanka. Faculty of Social Sciences at South Asian University, New Delhi Presents Contributions to Contemporary Knowledge Lecture Series – 2013.

Obeyesekere, Gananath. (2017). Between Portuguese and the Nayakas: the many faces of the Kandyan Kingdom, 1591-1765, Sr Lanka at the Crossroads of History, Z Biedermann and A Strathern (ed. 1917).

Obeyesekere, Gananath. (2017). The Doomed King, Sailfish Colombo, 2017.

Obeyesekere, Gananath. (2019). On Mundukondapola: Resurrecting the History of a Defunct Kingdom. Sri Lanka Journal of Sociology Vol-01 – 2019.

Obeyesekere, M. (2016). Kanda Udarata Samaja sanwidanaya saha Prabhuwaru, 2016, Samanthi Prakashakayo, Jaela.

Peiris, Edmond. (1947). The Maga Salakuna. The Journal of the Ceylon Branch of the Royal Asiatic Society of Great Britain & Island. Vol. 37. No. 104. PP 205-220.

Pollock, Sheldon (26 April 2016). A Rasa Reader: Classical Indian Aesthetics. Columbia University Press. p. 48. ISBN 978-0-231-54069-8.

Raghavan, MD (1964). India in Ceylonese History, Society and Culture. Indian Council for Cultural Relations Mew Delhi* 1964.

Raghavan, MD (1964a). Tamil culture in Ceylon: A general Introduction, Indian Council for Cultural Relations Mew Delhi* 1964.

Raghavan, MD. (1961). Karawa of Ceylon: Society and Culture, KVG De Silva & Sons, Colombo. 1961.

Rajakaruna, Shakila. (2021). Mahanuwara samaye puskola lekana rachana kirima ho karawima pinisa tathkalina sedahawathun meheyavunu agamika iganvim kipayak. 11 - 03 Volume, ISSN 2279-2020. Jathika Pusthakala ha Pralekana Seva Mandalaya.

Ray, Suchismita. (2022), The Rasa and Literary criticism in Sanskrit Poetics. International journal of creative research thoughts. © 2022 IJCRT | Volume 10, Issue 4 April 2022 | ISSN: 2320-2882

Sannasgala, P (1964) Sinhala Sahithya Wansaya. Lakehouse Printers. Colombo.

Sastri, Krishna H. (1916). South Indian Images of Gods and Goddesses. Madras Government Press.

Somadasa, KD (1993). Catalogue of the Hugh Nevill Collection of Sinalese Manuscripts in the British Library. Volume 5. The British Library.

Sugathawansa, Rev. Hatharabage. (215). Pali Sandesha Sahithya. Godage Brothers, Colombo.

Sumanajothi, Degammada (1966). Theruwan Mala. Colombo.

Suraweera, AV. (2014). The Rajavaliya: An Account of the Rulers of Sri Lanka and the First Ever Translation of the Alakesvara Yuddhaya

Thabrew, Vvian De. (2017). Poems of Nature in Sandesha Poetry. Godage Brothers, Colombo.

Thilakasiri, S. (2005). Sinhala Sandesha Kavyaye Deshapalana Pasubima. Godage Brothers, Colombo.

Thilakasiri, S. (2008). Sinhala Sandesha Kavyaye Samaja Pasubima. Godage Brothers, Colombo.

Thilakasiri, S. (2013). Sandesha Kavyaye saha Sahithya. Godage Brothers, Colombo.

Thilakasiri, Siri. (2013). Sandesha Kāvya Sahithya, S Godage Publishers, Colombo.

Wajirajnana Horana. (1992). Sinhala Sahithya Grantha Pradipika. Colombo.

www.sreenivasaraos.com/tag/Kāvya-alamkara-sutra-vritti

www.wisdomlib.org/definition

Appendix 4:
About the author

Bandara Bandaranayake Completed his B.Ed. (Honours) Degree and MPhil Degree at University of Colombo. He completed his PhD at Monash University on a Monash Graduate Scholarship.

After his first degree, he joined the Ministry of Education in Sri Lanka and held several teaching and senior administrative positions. After completing his PhD, and after a short tenure at Monash University, he joined the public service. He held several senior positions at the Department of Internal Affairs (New Zealand), the Department of Innovation, Industry and Regional Development (Australia), and the Department of Education and Training (Australia) for nearly three decades.

His research interests are in educational governance, public sector ethics and integrity, public policy analysis, cultural anthropology, social psychology and evolutionary psychology. He has published several books and number of journal articles.

He is currently engaged in independent research, consultancy, and counselling.

He can be contacted on bandaranayakeb@gmail.com.

www.ingramcontent.com/pod-product-compliance
Lightning Source LLC
Chambersburg PA
CBHW050941050726
47592CB00007B/2383